The
Falling Leaf

by

Trevor A. Smith

United Kingdom Territory of The Salvation Army
101 Newington Causeway
London SE1 6BN

© The General of The Salvation Army
First Published in the United Kingdom 2004
ISBN 0 85412 729 1

After training at The Salvation Army's William Booth College, Denmark Hill, London, Trevor Smith envisaged nothing more than a pastoral ministry at local Salvation Army centres. But early on he was appointed as secretary to a succession of national and international leaders. During other periods he headed young people's work in the Norwich, Canterbury and Ireland Divisions and later became Assistant National Youth Secretary. Leadership of the Army's work in the Sheffield Division was followed in 1985 by pioneering the Services to the Community Department at the Army's national headquarters for the UK and Ireland. Though faced with many tasks, one immediate concern was ministry to people affected by HIV/Aids, an involvement that later resulted in it becoming an appointment in its own right.

Trevor Smith has sought to ensure his calling to minister to people was practised in all appointments. Retirement has afforded opportunity to respond to The Salvation Army's invitation to write about his ministry to people affected by HIV/Aids in the United Kingdom, particularly during the early years of the pandemic. Though by nature a reserved person and conscious of his limitations, he has been thankful that God has seen fit to use him.

Cover design by Major Bruce Tulloch
Produced by THQ Literary Unit
Printed by Halstan & Co Ltd

CONTENTS

Chapter   **Page**

Dedication

This book is dedicated to God,
who used even me in ministry to people
— people from whom I received inspiration, challenge,
education, love and friendship —
and to The Salvation Army that supported this ministry.

FOREWORD

FROM THE BISHOP OF OXFORD
The Rt Reverend Richard Harries DD FKC FRSL
Diocesan Church House
North Hinksey
Oxford OX2 0NB

Trevor Smith has spent a lifetime serving the needy through The Salvation Army. Since 1985 the main focus of his ministry has been with people affected by HIV/AIDS. In this personal reminiscence he reflects on how he became involved and the people he has met and become friends with over the years. Written in an accessible style, with pen portraits of people and touches of humour it conveys well the truth that where the most vulnerable are, there is Jesus.

The author's approach has been entirely non-judgmental and he emphasises how much he has received from those he has been privileged to befriend and minister to.

Acknowledgements

Grateful thanks are due to many people but in particular to The Salvation Army of the United Kingdom for commissioning this book. And to David Dalziel for undertaking editorial work, giving much appreciated advice, suggestions for further improvement, corrections of the manuscript and processing the final outcome to the publishers.

Also thanks to people inside and outside of the Army for prayer, encouragement and in some instances scrutinising the chapters.

A special word of thanks to relations, friends and partners who have readily approved mention of loved ones and in some instances given additional information and photographs. This is reflected by a mother who writes, 'I must say it gave me overwhelming pleasure to know that you had remembered Kevin and that he wasn't just a statistic. I feel sure he would think it an honour to be a participant in your venture and I wish you all the luck in the world getting it published'.

And finally to you, dear reader, who I hope will glean from this modest book something to inform, inspire and be a source of prayerful and practical support of people here and overseas engaged in the care of people with HIV/Aids, their loved ones and friends.

God bless you!

1.

In Perspective

MUCH of the Peak District National Park and Derbyshire Dales were on my patch as leader of The Salvation Army's work in South Yorkshire, though there was little time to enjoy such delights. It was the time of the miners' strike. We were careful not to take sides, but tried to minister to needy miners' families, many in our own congregations being among them. In those demanding times I was more than grateful for supportive colleagues and warm-hearted hospitable Yorkshire people – all the more appreciated as I am a single man!

One day, while busy in my Pinstone Street office in Sheffield, a telephone call from London intimated a change of appointment. My mind went into overdrive! After three demanding but fulfilling years it was a case of leaving everything in readiness for my successor, plus all the upheaval entailed in moving house. Having been fully absorbed in the task at hand, it was a wrench to leave, and a surprise to be called back to London to pioneer a new 'Services to the Community' department.

This new department brought together a number of existing services, and some interesting people: Doreen James – responsible for the Nurses' Fellowship and an association for people with disabilities; Olive Bottle – busily engaged with the League of Mercy that includes hospital visitation throughout the country alongside other aspects of caring ministry, and a team of colleagues who worked industriously fulfilling many other essential tasks.

I wore a number of 'hats'.

As National Emergency Officer, I organised the Army's response with canteens and other support in times of national and local disasters. The Zeebrugge ferry disaster in March 1987 was particularly demanding, with the need for teams at Dover, Gatwick Airport and London, as well as responding to newspaper, radio and television interviews.

In 1986 we celebrated the centenary of Goodwill Work, a work amongst the most needy which Hugh Redwood wrote about long ago in his book *God in the Slums*. Big festivals in Bradford, Bristol and London Regent Hall were followed by a service in Southwark Cathedral, with HRH Princess Margaret as principal guest and Lord Tonypandy, formerly Mr Speaker, as guest speaker.

For a brief period I even had responsibility for Salvation Army work among servicemen in the United Kingdom. Sometimes I went out on the canteen serving refreshments on the firing ranges at Farnborough. Shades of the Army's work on the front line during the Second World War!

Another task was to organise soup-runs to the homeless, particularly in London. Robert Street, Editor of *The War Cry*, backed endeavours with an appeal for money to purchase sleeping bags. A generous public responded magnificently, enabling the purchase of lorry loads of sleeping bags from premises in Manchester. These were brought to London for use and distributed to other areas of the country as need arose.

A call came to go to the Ministry of Agriculture, Fisheries and Food to meet the Minister, John Gummer. He asked us to accept responsibility for the 'Common Market Food Operation'. Butter, ghee, beef and cheese were distributed throughout the country by ourselves and a number of other charities in an endeavour to reduce the so-called food mountains. We discouraged distribution of beef as we did not possess refrigerated transport and I was anxious about food poisoning. On reflection, that was fortunate in view of the later news about BSE.

In 1987 we were able to state that, excluding Scotland, invoices for cheese totalled in excess of £9 million, plus invoices for the other products. The United Kingdom did more than any other European country and the Army distributed more than any other charity. The huge task nearly brought about my breakdown. A book could be written about the food operation!

As if my colleagues and I were not coping with enough, Aids came into the picture. At that time I had become aware of the need to respond to the growing HIV/Aids pandemic. In 1986 I became involved in ministry to one person with Aids. As years passed, that commitment entailed supporting many more people until in 1991 my appointment was changed to Director: Aids Support Service.

The Army's 'Aids' ministry has always been in line with our policy to offer practical and pastoral support, in a non-judgemental manner, irrespective of how people contract the virus.

This book relates something of my personal involvement in Aids ministry. It's not a medical essay. You won't find details about how HIV/Aids is contracted or prevented. It gives neither medical case histories nor the latest information about the Human Immunodeficiency Virus (HIV) and Acquired Immune Deficiency Syndrome (Aids) nor how it is treated. Hospital clinics, the Terrence Higgins Trust, and other statutory and voluntary organisations have an abundance of information which is available if needed.

I make no claims to being a learned theologian, but simply reflect on the love and grace of God, self-evident in the lives of people with whom I have been involved. With the exception of chapter two, rather than a chronological list of experiences since 1985, you will find comparatively brief chapters dealing with issues encountered in the course of ministry.

Pastoral case histories are used to illustrate the theme of each chapter. In the main, first names only are used, although in many instances surnames are public knowledge. Every endeavour has been made to contact and gain the approval of all those concerned, either the people mentioned or – more often – loved ones or relatives who are left. In the main, case histories have their own lessons from which one can learn, without the author engaging in discussion. Written from a personal perspective, any views expressed are my own.

A strong connection between HIV infection and the gay community was the reality of those early pioneering years of the 1980s and the early 1990s. Some readers may have a problem in coping with so many case histories dealing with gay men. However, Jon, a gay man up front about his illness, used to remark:

> If you have a problem with me having Aids, it's your problem.
> Don't make it mine. I've enough to cope with.

Many haemophiliacs became HIV positive as a result of contaminated blood supplies, but I was not personally involved with any. Thankfully, as a result of advances in medical treatment in recent years, people are living much longer but Aids remains a potentially life-threatening illness, so there is no room for complacency.

The book contains a touch of humour and it is hoped this lightens the subject matter. The intention is to inform, inspire and enlighten – leading to a greater appreciation of the words of the Lord Jesus Christ: 'When I was ill you came to my help' (Matthew 25:36 *NEB*). I have generally tried to avoid using Salvation Army jargon, though 'The Army' is often used instead of 'The Salvation Army'. Aids is used in preference to AIDS. 'Gay' – Good As You – is used rather than homosexual. It's fewer letters to type!

Ranks and positions are not used, with just one or two exceptions. 'General' (the international leader of the Army) is used, not least because this is the only 'rank' bestowed by election rather than by appointment. The procedure is similar to that employed in electing a Pope. The main difference is that either a man or woman can be chosen!

The Army ministers to people with HIV/Aids in many lands. Methods are adapted to local cultures, which often include an emphasis on community education and change. My own ministry has been confined to the United Kingdom, mostly centred within the London area. It is for others to write about the Army's international HIV/Aids ministry.

Anyone reading this book will realise I have had a lot to deal with personally, including issues relating to the spiritual journey, death and bereavement, faith and the afterlife. Now in retirement, I reflect on over 40 years service as a Salvation Army officer, with appointments in widely differing spheres of service, all of which have brought fulfilment, not least the last appointment. Though I've tried to minister in God's name to other people, they have been the means by which God has ministered to me. Association with patients and partners, friends and relations, medical staff and so many others involved in the pastoral and caring professions, has immeasurably enriched my life.

I pay credit to staff at SA headquarters, officers and lay people, who throughout the years have backed and supported this ministry, not least with their prayers.

The ministry to people affected by HIV/Aids could be summed up in the words of a song by Albert Orsborn in *The Song Book of The Salvation Army* which speaks of service in the name of Jesus Christ –

I must love thee, love must rule me,
Springing up and flowing forth
From a childlike heart within me,
Or my work is nothing worth.
Love with passion and with patience,
Love with principle and fire,
Love with heart and mind and utterance,
Serving Christ my one desire.

2.

Leadership

– response to the growing crisis

THE year 1981 saw a number of people in the United States of America die of illnesses associated with a breakdown in the immune system, which came to be known as Acquired Immune Deficiency Syndrome – AIDS. Towards the end of the year the first person diagnosed as having Aids was confirmed in a London hospital. Many more were to follow.

June 1985

I had become increasingly aware of the Aids pandemic that, like a tidal wave, was beginning to affect the United Kingdom, little realising it would soon engulf me in ministry to people affected.

Following a call to the department, my colleague Elsie Grassham, an ardent hospital visitor, responded to a request from Charing Cross Hospital to visit one of their patients. Elsie had been a volunteer in the wards of St Christopher's Hospice for 12 years, so was used to such ministry. She discovered the young man, James, was from a Salvationist family, was at present in full-time employment, but that he had Aids and this made his future at that point in the pandemic rather grim.

Elsie would gladly have continued visiting but was relieved when I offered. This accelerated my education and involvement in Aids ministry! Becoming pastor, carer and friend, my visits continued in and out of hospital until eventually I took James to live with his mother. Not long after, I was deeply moved to be conducting his funeral – the first of all too many funerals I would conduct in the future. It was not only a bereavement for the family but also for me as a friend.

Despite public ignorance, fear and hostility surrounding this 'new' disease, I knew in my heart the Army's role was to come alongside the marginalised, whoever they were, in line with Christ's teaching and example and the traditional response of the Army to people in need. The Army's Medical Adviser, Dr Paul du Plessis, remarked in a letter, 'We do have a particular calling to the outcast and marginalised of our society and for this reason I fully agree that we should see those afflicted with Aids as part of our responsibility.'

October 1986

With my practical experience of caring for James, I thought it wise to alert colleagues to the new menace of Aids.

After consultation with Paul du Plessis, an A4 sheet was sent to colleagues throughout the country, headed *Pastoral Guidelines – Acquired Immune Deficiency Syndrome – AIDS*. It was among the first documents about Aids to be issued by a Christian denomination in this country.

Further guidelines were sent to the Army's leaders throughout the land in regard to members who might contract HIV and develop Aids. There was concern that measures should not be taken against anyone solely because they had contracted the illness. Any measures taken were to be on the basis of existing guidelines about conduct unbecoming of a Salvationist which were applicable to all members.

February 1987

The Chief of the Staff, Caughey Gauntlett, convened a meeting of international and national Salvation Army leaders at International Headquarters to debate the Army's response to the Aids pandemic. Dr Patrick Dixon of ACET – Aids Care Education & Training – and Dr Paul du Plessis addressed the company.

The large crowd present sensed the Army was facing a new and demanding challenge both here and in the many countries in which it ministers. Aids was viewed from a social as well as medical perspective, with increasing awareness of the need to offer hope to people in despair. The overwhelming response was positive. Those present saw this as an opportunity to respond to people in need, including those ostracised by society, and were determined that we should not 'pass by on the other side' (Luke 10:31, 32).

An American leader pleaded with tears in his eyes that our response to the pandemic should be compassionate, rather than judgmental.

It was agreed that the Army principle was to offer practical and pastoral support to all people, in a non-judgmental manner, irrespective of how they contracted the virus. As a consequence of this meeting, Caughey Gauntlett wrote to the national leader, Francy Cachelin –

> Perhaps the great difference with Aids is that it represents a moral and ethical question and it is here that the pastoral care needs to be of a very sensitive nature so as not to involve any judgmentalism.

Later in the month, eight of us met in Caughey Gauntlett's office for further discussion. One of the outcomes was that I was charged with responsibility for drafting a booklet on the subject of Aids.

November 1987

Following exhaustive correspondence and discussions with many people, *Aids Care – Practical and Pastoral Guidelines* was published (see page 37). The initial print run of 5,000 soon sold out and a further 5,000 had to be printed, selling both in the UK and overseas.

March 1990

Dr Ian Campbell succeeded Paul as the Army's Medical Adviser. He drew upon a wealth of experience in Aids work from his time as Medical Director of the Army's Chikankata Hospital, Zambia, to extend the Army's worldwide ministry to people with Aids.

June 1991

Ian organised an international conference on Aids, held at the Army's hotel in Leysin, Switzerland, where 114 delegates, 16 of them doctors, were brought together from 28 countries for intensive discussion, worship and setting of goals. It was a touchstone for the further development of the Army's international Aids programme.

Among the delegates was José, a young Salvationist with Aids, from Brazil. In the city of Brazilia, he was involved in one of the poorest areas as president of the Rainbow Project. Rank and status did not belong to José, yet he was an outstanding leader. His first language was Portuguese but in faltering English he dictated his testimony to me, part of which reads:

> I started to work with people with Aids long before I knew about my result. I have always felt in my heart and spirit the desire to do something for people.
> In the group with which I am working I am in contact every day with those who are dying. I have lost five friends in the last few months. It has been a tremendous burden for me. I try through the contact I

have with the people to offer the hope that I have in Jesus but I know also that my death may be near. I accompanied a friend during seven months and he was well advanced with Aids. He had no hope and did not believe in anything. I started to speak of Jesus and of the hope and peace he could give him. During this time he started to open himself to me. Later he went into hospital and the doctors said he had only one week to live. A nurse friend telephoned and asked me to come quickly because the fellow was going to die. I went and found he was at the door of death. There were four more patients with him, seemingly not so serious. During the week they all died but my friend did not die and gradually he became a bit better and was at that time speaking of the Lord Jesus, hoping to leave hospital. One day before he was due to leave hospital he took his own life, throwing himself from the 8th floor. I was distressed because I had invested a lot in his life. This has helped me speak more with my friends about Jesus and the hope that he gives.

At the Swiss conference, concern for José's well-being found expression during a meeting. He was invited to kneel in the centre of the room. Delegates formed a prayer circle round him, those in the centre laying their hands on him. Everyone was deeply moved in prayer for José. Before returning to Brazil, he spent three days in London, hosted

PHOTO: ROBIN BRYANT

José with Andrew and Vivienne (left) and Trevor, Leysin

by Andrew and Vivienne Wileman at Wandsworth. This enabled him to share fellowship, to see London and to gain some further insights into Aids work.

On one of the three days, we went to the Kobler Centre where José had blood tests, the results of which I sent him nine days later. He was supposed to have tests every six months but had not had one for a year. This visit was all the more appreciated as it was essential for him to know how much further HIV had affected his immune system. The modern centre, the helpfulness of the staff, and the fact that I knew many in the crowd of patients attending this outpatient clinic impressed him. Visits to London Lighthouse, Body Positive, Mildmay Mission Hospital and Westminster Hospital followed. Visits to my friends Colin and also Michael, both of whom had Aids, concluded the tour. All the visits made a tremendous impression upon him. A busy but worthwhile day!

After arriving back in Brazil, José maintained contact and some of us, including Wandsworth Oasis, were glad to help towards the cost of his treatment.

In one of his letters, translated, he writes –

My birthday was a very special and happy day. You know why? Your letter wishing me a happy birthday arrived and was the only one I received. Thank you for this, for the £30 and for the flag with the colours of the rainbow. My friends from the Rainbow Project were happy with the present and the flag has already been used on a few occasions to express hope and life.

Writing in October 1995 when for a period he lived a long distance from Brasilia before returning to the city, José states,

I am alone in my troubles. I have hardly received any pastoral care and I'm facing great difficulties at the moment. I very much need prayer. I'm not finding anyone to be at my side and help in my conflicts. The Army's officers who do care for me and always support me live a distance of 38 hours travel away from me but they give support through phone calls. These past few years I have faced many difficulties. 1993/94 was a year of great losses. I lost my best friend who died of heart failure and my sister who died of cancer. I suffered a great deal. This was alongside financial difficulties (the cost of medication). In a storm strong winds destroyed half of my roof. It was awful but the Lord gave me peace and patience and I eventually sorted it all out.

Thankfully the Reverend Luiz Caetano, the Diocesan Anglican General Secretary, translated the letter from José and I learned that

Caroline Batey, an Anglican English missionary nurse also was supportive of him. As time went by and health declined, José's letters make heart-breaking reading, yet they reflect his strong faith and resilient spirit. Extracts from the letters were shared with a group that was supporting him financially and in prayer.

He died in 1997 but not before he had a long article of testimony, similar to the one he had dictated to me, published in a national newspaper in Brazil. His was leadership of the highest order.

John Hunter Clinic

In the early years of the Aids pandemic, Senior Registrar Dr Charles Farthing and his colleagues pioneered Aids work at the John Hunter Clinic, to which many people resorted for counselling, testing and treatment, in the old St Stephen's Hospital. The hospital opened in 1878 as St George's Union Infirmary. It became St Stephen's in 1925, a change suggested by Kenneth Watters, later the husband of Enid Blyton, who was a surgeon in the hospital.

First impressions were of a forbidding place but modest building improvements and, more particularly, the staff made the atmosphere in the clinic warm and welcoming. Patient stress was, understandably, a very real factor, so everything possible was done to ensure a welcoming atmosphere, with pleasant décor, plants and music, and seating arrangements conducive to quietness or – if desired – conversation with other people. In this setting, where it seemed that everything possible was already being done, and medical expertise, new research, new drugs, new treatments were of paramount importance it was very reassuring when Charles said to me one day with some urgency in his voice:

Trevor, we need you, we need the Army to be involved in responding to this pandemic.

That simple, urgent statement, that word of encouragement has remained with me and inspired me through the years. Those were years when ignorance, fear and prejudice were rife, as was reflected in the film *Philadelphia* that starred Tom Hanks. Medications for the illness were few and mostly brought only short-term relief. News from around the world of supposed healing medications and cures raised the hope of individuals who sought to acquire them but all too often had their hopes dashed. Frequently such claims of healing were made by people seeking to make a fast buck or desiring publicity. Thankfully, nowadays medication gives greater hope of significantly extending life expectancy.

Public figures

A number of public figures played their part in raising awareness of Aids. There is no doubt that Diana, Princess of Wales, gave leadership at a time of great fear, ignorance and hostility to people with Aids. To be featured in the media holding the hands of a person with Aids sent out a clear message to the population, the Church included, that it was wrong to cut Aids patients off from everyday contact.

And she also did much behind the scenes, without publicity.

The then Archbishop of Canterbury, Robert Runcie, readily went to hospitals and met staff and patients, quietly chatting with them and praying with those who appreciated such visits. Cardinal Basil Hume, too, visited patients and staff and gave grants to support the ministry of care to people with Aids. It was not uncommon to see him in Westminster Hospital, even during a busy Easter weekend. He would stroll into the ward, simple staff in hand, to visit patients and give them his blessing.

Diana, Princess of Wales with Colin.
See pages 88-92 and colour plates

In the late 1980s, General Eva Burrows, international leader of the Army, became a patron of ACET – Aids Care Education & Training. It reflected her interest in developing the Army's worldwide ministry to people with Aids. I went with her one afternoon, visiting people with Aids and those in a supportive role. Some time was spent with colleagues at the Army's centre in Chelsea, visiting several people with Aids in a nearby flat, and visiting patients, friends, carers, volunteers and staff in the Westminster Hospital. Making maximum use of the time, Michael, a former Salvationist and member of Body Positive, joined us in the car, enabling him to converse further with the General. A report in Salvationist helped to encourage Salvationists to become involved in a ministry to people living with Aids. Leadership of the various voluntary Aids organisations in London and elsewhere has been crucial. Some people have themselves had Aids and are no more with us, but they have left pioneering work that stands to their credit.

Diana, Princess of Wales, Memorial Lecture

The National Aids Trust has been at the forefront of leadership and policy making, and the mutual support of Chief Executive, Derek Bodell (now succeeded by Deborah Jack) has been appreciated. As a result, I was able to go to the Bank of England in June 1999 to hear UN Secretary-General, Kofi Annan, deliver the first Diana, Princess of Wales, Memorial Lecture on Aids. It was an enriching experience to listen to this great statesman. The National Aids Trust report on the event states:

> The Financial Times and The Lancet both focused on the challenges for the business community as laid out by the Secretary-General: the need to develop and implement strategies to protect HIV-infected workers and their families from discrimination; the promotion of awareness and prevention campaigns within their workforces and local communities, and the need for business to think about HIV from a global perspective.

In December 2001, former President of the United States of America, Bill Clinton, delivered the Diana, Princess of Wales Lecture on Aids, in the Queen Elizabeth II Centre, accompanied by his wife and his daughter, who was studying in England at the time. He likewise exhibited a breadth and depth of knowledge of the subject that was impressive. He was obviously concerned that governments and businesses throughout the world should heed the impact of the pandemic, which was cutting a swathe particularly through the working populations of developing countries, putting the economies of such countries in jeopardy.

Edwin Cameron, Justice of the Supreme Court of South Africa, delivered the December 2003 lecture, in the City Hall, London. He was listened to with rapt attention. The National Aids Trust described him as:

> . . . a distinguished campaigner for the rights of people with HIV and Aids . . . who is himself living with HIV, has taken a bold and unparalleled stance in making public his diagnosis, and, as such has been an inspiration to many people around the world who are seeking better support in the fight against HIV and Aids.

Ecumenical and Parliamentary

The Very Reverend Michael Mayne, former Dean of Westminster Abbey, gave leadership in chairing meetings of the London Ecumenical Aids Forum, held in the historic Jerusalem Chamber of the Abbey. In addition, he occasionally invited people living with Aids and their carers to join with him in the evening for refreshments in the Jerusalem Chamber. Then he would lead everyone in a tour of the Abbey, when doors were closed to the public, concluding with evening prayers in the simplicity of the Chapel of St Faith – a profoundly moving and memorable experience.

I would often meet Mrs Daphne Rae JP on her visits to patients in Westminster Hospital. Daphne facilitated my attendance at meetings of the All Party Parliamentary Group on Aids, chaired by Lord Kilmarnock. It was an opportunity to hear learned guest speakers and in conversation and correspondence acquaint parliamentarians and other people about the Army's ministry in this and other lands.

Although the meetings are now held in private, those that other invited guests and I attended proved useful. The leadership of parliamentarians continues to have an influence for good.

Army's Principles

I was in The Netherlands when in 1987 a hurricane swept through England, felling countless trees and damaging many properties. I had gone there with the Chief of the Staff and Mrs Ron Cox – who had previously been stationed in that country – for the Army's European Community Workers' Conference.

While there, Willem van der Harst, in charge of the Army's centre in the red light district of Amsterdam, took me to see David Stein, a leader and psychologist associated with a gay and lesbian health organisation. There, in his lovely home, I was able to thank him for reminding the community that, whatever their reservations about the Army, it should be remembered that it was one of the first organisations to respond to people in need.

I was able to assure him of the Army's principles in regard to supporting people with HIV/Aids. On return to the red light district centre a colleague came back from hospital to report that a young man was dying as a result of Aids and wanted the officer to visit him.

Timely evidence of the Army's policy.

13

3.

God's Wrath?

– hospitals and attitudes

'WHAT do you want?' demanded the competent but anxious charge nurse on Thomas Macaulay Ward in the old St Stephen's Hospital, Fulham Road, London. She was concerned to safeguard the interests of patients, as well-intentioned but misguided people had tried to get on to the ward to warn patients that they were experiencing 'God's wrath' for their sins and should repent. True, there is need to call on all people to repent of their sins and seek forgiveness – but there is a right and a wrong way of engaging in the ministry of reconciling men and women to God. Thankfully, Clive Carswell SRN had already shown me round the ward and introduced me to patients, so I was able to explain that this was a follow-up visit to patients who wanted to see me again.

There was another reason for the visit. Grenville Burn had received a generous donation of Trebor Softmints on behalf of the Army and, as he was a staunch supporter of my varied ministry at that time, he gave me a quantity. These were distributed to patients and hard-working nurses, who much appreciated the gesture.

Much of my involvement has been with St Stephen's Hospital. When it was demolished and the work moved to Westminster Hospital, I likewise moved. Later, the Chelsea & Westminster Hospital was built on the Fulham Road site and became a flagship hospital of the National Health Service. The work returned to that site and resulted in the closure of the old Westminster Hospital.

Due to my support of so many people, I have also had a lot to do with Mildmay Mission Hospital, particularly in the earlier years. This has also been true of London Lighthouse, when they had a residential unit. My ministry has involved visiting people with Aids in Charing Cross Hospital, St Bartholomew's Hospital, St Mary's Hospital, Middlesex

Hospital and a number of other hospitals and hospices. In them all, I have been glad to co-operate and be supportive of medical staff, particularly during the early years of the Aids pandemic.

Most patients have been young and articulate, many of them professional people, often earning a good wage. Particularly in the early years, when the medical profession was also on a learning curve, such patients were not afraid to challenge doctors. Many knew as much as – if not more than – some medical staff about the new virus which was killing their contemporaries. Such challenges came to be regarded positively, and resulted in a more consultative process, with doctors placing options before patients and patients deciding which options to accept.

This policy came to be the means of establishing more respectful, trusting and friendly relationships between medical staff, including doctors, and patients. In many instances, use of Christian names became the norm enabling barriers to be broken down between staff and patients.

Ward 5B

Randy Shilts's book *And The Band Played On* (ISBN 0670822701) is a masterpiece of investigative journalism. Published by St Martin's Press in 1987, it relates the impact of HIV/Aids in the United States of America. Shilts's reference to Ward 5B, the Aids Ward of San Francisco General Hospital, makes significant reading:

> All the nurses were volunteers. About half were gay men and the other half were women. All had undergone extensive encounter sessions to examine their sentiments about death and dying. Cliff Morrison, a gay clinical nurse specialist, organised and designed the ward as he saw fit, because the more important hospital administrators all seemed rather embarrassed by the ward and the disease. The thirty-two-year-old Morrison was a dedicated idealist who disliked the hierarchical doctor-nurse-patient model that dominated hospitals. Doctors would not run this ward; he would, and he wouldn't even call himself head nurse, preferring instead the less authoritative moniker (title) of nursing co-ordinator. Patients would have a louder voice in their own care, which only made sense, Morrison noted, because they usually knew more about the intricacies of their often experimental medications than their doctors … Morrison also rejected the idea of visiting hours as a concept designed for the convenience of nurses rather than patients, and he instituted policies to permit visitors to stay overnight if they wished.

I cannot speak for the rest of the country but similar policy changes in some of the London hospital wards I visited were immediately seen to make a positive contribution to the physical and psychological wellbeing of patients and their loved ones.

In my youth, when I was in the family business, we used to say 'The customer comes first'. Such a policy in regard to patients is a principle to be commended for hospitals as a whole, not just to wards dedicated to the care of people with Aids. After all, it is the patients who 'pay the piper.' Come to think of it, the dictums 'The customer comes first' and 'We aim to please' may have limitations but they could be recommended to other industries, particularly service industries, including the medical profession.

Centre spread of Scriptographic
pamphlet
About Caring for People with
Aids
see page 37

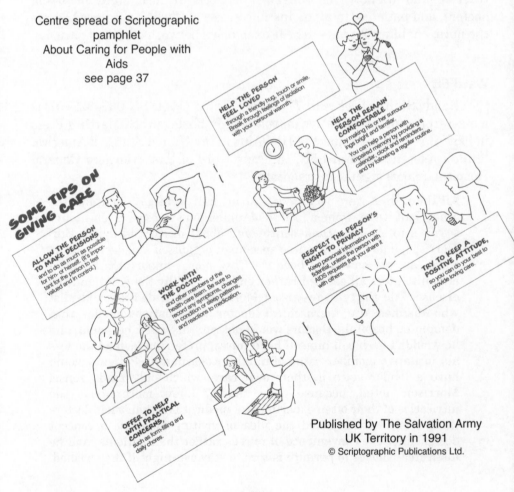

SOME TIPS ON GIVING CARE

HELP THE PERSON FEEL LOVED
through a friendly hug, touch or smile. Break through feelings of isolation with your personal warmth.

HELP THE PERSON REMAIN COMFORTABLE
by making his or her surroundings bright and familiar. You can help a person with impaired memory by providing a calendar, clock and reminders, and by following a regular routine.

ALLOW THE PERSON TO MAKE DECISIONS
and to do as much as possible for him- or herself. (It's important for the person to feel valued and in control.)

WORK WITH THE DOCTOR
and other members of the health-care team. Be sure to record any symptoms, changes in condition or sleep patterns, and reactions to medication.

RESPECT THE PERSON'S RIGHT TO PRIVACY
Keep personal information confidential, unless the person with AIDS requests that you share it with others.

TRY TO KEEP A POSITIVE ATTITUDE,
so you can do your best to provide loving care.

OFFER TO HELP WITH PRACTICAL CONCERNS,
such as form-filling and daily chores.

Published by The Salvation Army
UK Territory in 1991
© Scriptographic Publications Ltd.

4.

Wheelchairs and Wobblies

IT WAS always a joy to take Jonathan out in his wheelchair. He'd laugh, joke and giggle about so many things, looking with fascination into shop windows, embraced by the hustle and bustle of the busy street and the rush of impatient traffic.

Grandad taking grandson for a cheery walk?

No, me taking dear Jonathan, a full-grown man so weakened by Aids that he was obliged to use a wheelchair, from London Lighthouse, along the busy road around Ladbroke Grove, including the renowned market of Portobello Road. The bond between us was strong and I didn't begrudge the time spent with him on such jaunts. People little realised the heart-breaking joy that was mine, our laughs belying our tears.

To add to the joyous pain of such trips came the occasional pothole in the path or road, the uneasy camber or crack, the irregular so-called provision for wheelchairs which is supposed to enable them to pass easily from pavement to road, avoiding kerbs of Everest-seeming height. All this added further interest to my efforts to steer the wheelchair so that it did not run over the feet of old ladies, collide with inconsiderate pedestrians or injure dogs on leads. Negotiating shops with difficult access and tiny aisles increased the hazards encountered.

At times I think basic training for all those who construct or maintain roads and pathways should include a number of hours taking adults in wheelchairs round busy shopping streets. Training should also include politicians and financial decision-makers. If they haven't got the strength to do it as a driver, let them do it in the role of the disabled!

And Jonathan?

His story is elsewhere in this volume. Suffice to say he concluded his life in London Lighthouse, his well-proportioned physique blighted by the horrid blemishes of Kaposi's sarcoma, the whole of his face and eyes included. I have snapshots of him taken in those last days and I still find it difficult to look at them. Destroy them? I have wondered, yet somehow they come as a heart-breaking reminder of a fine, cheerful young man, who endured painful but hilarious journeys in a wheelchair.

Precious times, when true love as friends lingers awhile.

Yes, I have an interest in wheelchairs – or rather the people in them! I recently went to a demonstration of dance by students with disabilities at the National Star College, Ullenwood, near Cheltenham. Being on the Education and Student Welfare Committee of the Board of Governors, I had a particular involvement and interest in the activities of the college. Here young men and women in the 16 – 25 age group undertake advanced education that will enable them to live independent lives in the future. All of them have disabilities, some more extreme than others.

Dance, you say?

Well, obviously they can't dance in the manner engaged in by people without such disabilities. No, it was more akin to rhythmic movement, even as far as getting out of the wheelchair and doing the movements on the floor, drawing attention to the fact that they are people, not attachments to wheelchairs. Most of us have also seen such dance in one of those features that have replaced the image of the globe during intervals on BBC TV.

The Army has an association for people with disabilities and an annual residential week for them, when they engage particularly in instrumental music, united singing, timbrel playing, worship and fellowship. The week concludes with a festival in a gymnasium, to which friends and relations are invited, packing the place out. It's great!

In 1985, the leader at the time, Doreen James, invited me to the event at a college in Coventry. Though a lovely place, I thought we could do better, so took Doreen on a visit to the National Star College, in the beautiful setting of Ullenwood, and the event has taken place there ever since. I guess some people are tired of hearing about my involvement in that regard.

Colin

Dr David Holmes, now retired, had a great respect and affection for Colin and was always glad when I brought him to the clinic for treatment and, latterly, regular blood transfusions. I likewise had respect and affection for Colin. When leader of the Army's work in South Yorkshire, I

Trevor and Colin on board M/V San Miguel

became aware that Colin had at one time expressed a desire to enter our college and become an officer but for various reasons this interest had lapsed and he had moved away. I tracked him down to Glasgow and made a brief visit when on holiday in that great city. We retained a tenuous link after that visit.

One day an urgent call came from the family to say that Colin had been taken very seriously ill and was in the intensive care unit. I immediately went to be with him, taking it in turn with the family to sit with him for hours, holding his hand and talking into his ear, as he was being kept unconscious in order to facilitate his recovery. It was touch-and-go but he did recover and eventually returned home and to a demanding job. When declining health obliged him to give up work, Colin moved with his little dog to a flat. Support was all the more needed in those days, as this tall, good-looking young man was obliged to use a wheelchair.

Came the day when he wanted to go on an overseas holiday and both of us knew it was likely to be his last. At his request, I gladly accompanied him to Playa del Ingles in the Canary Islands.

He booked the transport and half-board at a hotel and we shared costs. Having made advance arrangements, we received excellent support from railway staff, who facilitated me pushing Colin in the wheelchair through the obstacle course on arrival and then on departure from the train. Arriving at the airport, we were again helped by staff, who sped us through all the checks and onto the aircraft before any other passengers boarded. It shows that by prior arrangements a lot can be done to facilitate travel for a person in a wheelchair.

We enjoyed a good hotel, with plenty of much needed food, and immediately after breakfast two places would be reserved beside the pool. Colin was by now developing very obvious purple blemishes of Kaposi's sarcoma all over his body but we would park the wheelchair by a nearby wall, strip off to bathing costumes and lie in the sun. I would pour protective oil and gently rub it all over his body, seeking during the morning to respond to his every need, such as fetching drinks. I admired his courage in not seeking to hide his thinness and purple blemishes from the looks of people nearby. When wheeling him back into the hotel, I did so with my nose in the air, proudly pushing him along and ignoring the glances of the curious.

One day I returned to the wheelchair placed against the wall to find an unused condom had been put on it. Someone mistakenly thought we were 'an item'! At least they saw the need for people to use condoms and practise safer sex.

Following a rest in the hotel during the afternoon and a good evening meal, in the darkness of the evening I would wheel Colin along the seafront and the busy shopping arcades before returning late to a good night's sleep. A coach trip round the island and a sail on the *M/V San Miguel* further enhanced what was for us a thoroughly enjoyable holiday. Colin generously bought thin gold neck chains for himself and for me. Though not a particularly expensive item, it was invested with sentimental value. Alas, at a later date when visiting a friend in Hackney, I was in civvies, wearing the chain and was mugged by three youths who wrenched it from my neck. I learned a hard lesson. Don't wear expensive-looking items, in an 'at risk district' and be heedful of who is nearby when walking along the street.

Along with his supportive family, I was heart-broken when Colin died, as I thought a lot of him. It was my sad privilege to conduct his funeral. Photographs of him continue to remind me of a Christian gentleman and friend.

5.

Mothers

SOME mothers, despite being bereaved of their sons, have committed themselves to continuing support of people affected by Aids. One such is Betty Feldman, who relates a little of her experience and of her faith as follows:

Betty Feldman

> When my son, Michael, was diagnosed as having Aids, many different thoughts crowded in on me. There was anger: Why my son? Why such a gentle, good person, who tried never knowingly to harm another human being?
>
> There was the feeling of wanting to try and avert whatever happens to people with the virus. After all, I was his mother and averting bad things to my children was part of my role in life. Then there was the thought that someone had made a mistake and the results were not those of Michael, that there must have been a mix-up.
>
> All these thoughts were for him – until I was alone with my thoughts and the biggest test of my life. Namely, how could I pray now when, all of a sudden, my anger towards God was so strong that I could not believe there was a God?
>
> I was brought up and lived my Jewish religion as far back as I could remember. It was part of daily life. My parents were orthodox Jews, so religion and faith were as normal to me as food. Then all of a sudden I felt cheated. I could not find a way to pray. What good would prayer do? I could not comfort Michael and tell him this was 'God's will.

21

Which God? What God? What will? This was sheer malice meted out to Michael and me by the so-called God. What had happened to the all-forgiving and gentle Father in Heaven? Most mothers have a particular sensitivity to the plight of their offspring, frequently taking the initiative in visiting and giving emotional and practical support. The commitment to care on the part of parents, particularly mothers, has been a lesson in itself. As a mother, it has been a privilege to associate with many of them.

This was probably one of the biggest hurdles I had to climb during this period and, let me confess, it took a long time to find some sort of answer which I could live with. It started with me praying while Michael was ill and then, all of a sudden, realising that this was what I was doing – praying.

I was acknowledging that there was a God. And, like a child, I found solace in the fact that, yes, there is a higher being. There are things that I can never understand, or forgive, but these are the facts of life. I realised I had been given in Michael a precious gift for 34 years and that I had no right to complain.

Maybe my believing took a big dive during this period but, equally, could I ever have weathered the bad times during and after Michael's sickness and death, if I did not have my faith restored?

I know now that I could not

Brian's mother

Following the death of a loved one, some families wish to retain contact with me through the following years, as I may be one of the few remaining links with their son. Contact with most families, however, abates after a while and this is understood as contact with me may revive painful memories of bereavement.

One person with whom I did maintain contact was Brian's mother, who used to converse with me at length in private. She had loved Brian dearly and after his death the depth of her heartache for him was obvious. Originating from the north of England, she went back home following her son's death but felt there was no one in whom she could confide. This added to her burden, for it was a time of ignorance, fear and hostility from some quarters of the population. She had no inclination to risk divulging any information about her son and her own heartache.

Right up to the time of her own death, whenever I had cause to visit the north of England I took the opportunity to call on Brian's mother to offer a listening ear and emotional support.

Impressive dignity

I have often been struck by the fact that Jesus was in the same age group as many people who have Aids. Just as mothers have been concerned for their offspring with Aids, so the mother of Jesus and other concerned women gathered, watching the Crucifixion:

> There stood by the cross of Jesus his mother, and his mother's sister, Mary the wife of Cleophas, and Mary Magdalene. When Jesus therefore saw his mother, and the disciple standing by, whom he loved, he saith unto his mother, Woman, behold thy son! Then saith he to the disciple, Behold thy mother! And from that hour the disciple took her unto his own home (John 19:25-27, *KJV*).

It was an honour to visit and be supportive of a young man in his home and, later, associate with his mother and friends when the funeral took place. The Jewish service was a learning experience, leaving me impressed with how the Rabbi sought to include everyone, whether Jews or not, so that we all had an understanding of what was taking place. After the moving service in the prayer hall, we followed the coffin on its plain, wooden trolley out to the burial place, where it was placed in the earth, followed by two large black polythene bags containing books. In correspondence with Rabbi Larry Tabick, I am advised that the books may not necessarily have been those of the deceased. He writes:

> Books with any of seven Hebrew names of God in them may not be destroyed; instead they are buried, often at funerals.

I joined with other men in shovelling soil into the grave, before we wended our way back to some running water where we ceremonially cleansed our hands. We all then individually and briefly extended our condolences to the bereaved mother, before departing. I was impressed with the dignity with which the mother bore herself, although her heart was breaking, and with the consolation brought by the service and the participation of everyone. A very moving event.

At the request of friends, I later conducted a brief memorial gathering in London Lighthouse.

Valerie

Mothers in particular feel the loss of a son or daughter, especially if they are miles away from their loved one and friends. As a mother herself, Valerie, a florist, has provided free of charge a little posy for bereaved mothers. To see a mother getting onto a train clutching such a posy was a moving scene. Those were precious moments, when 'saying it with flowers' was so significant. Since those times, Valerie has been obliged to sell her shop but maintains an interest in the ministry in which she had a significant part.

Jonathan

It was the Tuesday afternoon tea party of sandwiches and cakes, made available and served by a team of hospital volunteers. Patients, relations and friends had gathered in the day room of the ward in the old Westminster Hospital for a time of fellowship and food. 'Hey, Salvation Army, can you loan me five quid?' a young man in his twenties called from across the room. I never did get back those five pounds but my life was immeasurably enriched as through several years I supported Jonathan as he contended with his life-threatening illness.

He had been brought up in a children's home and had no mother or father or relations to whom he could introduce me. Jonathan had a flamboyant personality and zest and pace of life that even his contemporaries found difficult to match. Despite declining health, he was courageously determined to make the most of life, even when quite poorly taking to the floor of a club and showing everyone how to dance!

Although if there was cause he could give people the lashing of his tongue, Jonathan nevertheless had great generosity of spirit. He appreciated good nursing and on numerous occasions would buy flowers for the nursing staff, the last time being a huge floral arrangement from Harrods for the staff of London Lighthouse.

Educationally he had done particularly well in music and his love for this art enabled him to appreciate not only the latest popular but also classical music. It was on his initiative that we both attended a performance of *Messiah* in Westminster Abbey. On another occasion, Robert and I took him to a restaurant and, in spite of vomiting before the event, Jonathan was determined to go to the theatre and enjoy the musical *Les Misérables*.

Jonathan had few photographs of himself, except several from his younger years and a photo taken in later years for the purpose of the magazine *Gay Times*. Jonathan was good-looking and well endowed in every sense, so it made a good photograph of its type but not the sort that I could ultimately use on the front of an order of service!

Time came when the purple blemishes of Kaposi's sarcoma were already beginning to be evident in his face. He had no mother to chivvy him to have his photo taken.

I therefore took him to Robin Bryant's studio where an excellent portrait photograph was produced.

Although a popular person, during the final years of his life he had few really close friends. One friend, Robert, and I came close to Jonathan, seeking in various ways to be supportive of him. When first we met, he was living in a hostel but then secured a flat in the East End of London. It was very poorly heated and, not being in good health, he felt the cold all the more, so when it was bitterly cold he stayed at Robert's flat.

Conscious of declining health, Jonathan stayed at my flat during several very cold nights.

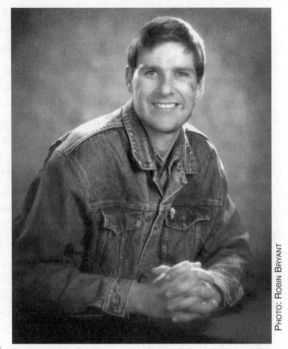

Jonathan

Tucking him up in bed one night, in the darkness of the room his plaintive voice came to me, 'Don't leave me, Trevor.' Hurt, lonely and ill, those words came from fathoms deep. I never did leave him, nor did Robert. In the truest sense of the word, we saw him through to the end, his prayer answered.

Staying at Robert's flat one evening, he was making up his pillbox for the week, each day and each section of the day having its horrific quantity of tablets and capsules. It was a daunting prospect to anticipate taking all those pills spread before him. The task suddenly blew his mind and he took a substantial overdose. One can only imagine what pushed him to that point of despair.

Robert immediately telephoned me and we rushed Jonathan to hospital where, after giving full details, we waited all too long for him to receive medical attention. Did the medical staff, who did not seem to be over-stretched with patients, think Jonathan was a drug addict and imagine he had overdosed? If so, they were very wrong. Ultimately he was pumped out and admitted to a ward. Next day, Jonathan became exasperated, so discharged himself and came home! Robert and I were glad to see him and looked after him as only friends can.

Thankfully, Jonathan eventually had a flat made available to him much nearer to where Robert lived. It was more attractive, warm and convenient for shops and transport. That one bedroom flat meant so much to him. Robert and I were only too glad to help him furnish the place and make it look good. Alas, he was not able to enjoy the flat as long as we had wished.

All too soon Jonathan was again admitted to hospital and, later, to the London Lighthouse residential unit, where he was cared for in a room of his own. Robert and I spent many hours with him, day after day. Wouldn't a mother have done the same? But there was no known mother.

When he recovered somewhat, I would take Jonathan in his wheelchair around the district, including the Portobello Road, as related in the chapter Wheelchairs and Wobblies.

He had a 'fighting spirit' and was determined to spend one more night at the flat that meant so much to him. Robert and I made all necessary preparations. Heating full on, bed nicely made, refreshments available if needed, even the oxygen cylinders and mask hired from Boots. Those few hours at home were a laugh in the face of death! He was brave, so courageous and strong in spirit; it called forth my highest admiration.

O death, where is thy sting? O grave, where is thy victory? The sting of death is sin; and the strength of sin is the law. But thanks be to God which giveth us the victory through our Lord Jesus Christ

(1 Corinthians 15:55-57, *KJV*).

Robert and I knew Jonathan's life was concluding and we were with him into the darkness of the night at London Lighthouse. Needing a brief break, we both went to the balcony and looked up at the clear starlit night. A bright moon shone down upon us. Words were unnecessary and we gave each other a hug, knowing the shared anguish that was ours. As we did so, an airliner from Heathrow passed across the face of the moon. Jonathan's spirit had also taken flight. He died aged 29 in 1991, surrounded by much love and, I believe, upheld by the love of God. I cannot say that Jonathan was particularly religious, yet when staying at my flat one night he had grabbed my Salvation Army song book. He quickly flicked through its pages and marked the songs he wanted at his funeral.

On another occasion, without prompting he had written a poem with the line 'So, God, watch by me close tonight and take my soul above.' According to his understanding, he was ready to depart this life for the next, knowing he was much loved not only by those of us who were his friends but also by the Lord, who said:

I will never leave thee, nor forsake thee (Hebrews 13:5, *KJV*).

Jonathan's funeral took place at Putney Vale Crematorium and afterwards Wandsworth Oasis provided a buffet meal in the Army's hall in Wandsworth. It was a celebration of Jonathan's life, just as he would have wished. For a while, Robert retained Jonathan's ashes in his own home. Later he passed them to me for safe keeping.

Robert

Inevitably, Robert and I had a lot to do with each other, not just because of our support for Jonathan but also because he, too, was not in the best of health. I gladly visited him and often his cat, Tara, would put on a display of excitement, racing from one end of the flat to the other.

Robert had a deep love for his mother, who took the long journey to visit him from time to time. It was always a pleasure to meet her and indulge in a meal at the local fish and chip shop. The shopkeeper purchased his fish from the market early each morning, so it was good to have fresh rather than frozen fish.

Although his health was declining, Robert was fiercely independent and, knowing how much his mother loved him, did not want her to be unduly worried and come to London, reside in his flat and take care of him. Despite my concern, he was adamant that his mother should not be urged to return to London.

Robert was finally in Westminster Hospital, where he so much appreciated the care of nursing staff, presenting them with two big floral arrangements from Valerie's the florist. He gave permission for his mother to be contacted, as he had become very poorly. I spent the early hours of the morning with him. The nurses gave him every attention until, having been washed, he sat in an armchair wearing his favourite denim clothes. 'Robert,' I said, 'I'm going off now to meet your mother at the station and bring her here to see you. God bless you, my love.'

And with that I gave him a gentle touch and departed.

I was away a comparatively short time but as his mother and I walked into the ward we immediately sensed something had happened.

We were ushered into a side room and informed that Robert had just died. It was heart-breaking to realise his mother had not seen him on that day just prior to his death, yet somehow perhaps that is what Robert wanted to happen, lest he see his mother's anguish waiting for him to die.

Two days later we went to the chapel of rest of J. H. Kenyon Ltd in the Westbourne Grove premises. Invited to pray, I did so with a shared sense of sorrow, then left Robert's mother there for a few moments of quietness before departing.

Robert, alas, died six months after Jonathan. Bearing my own sense of loss and, as his executor, I conducted his funeral at Putney Vale Crematorium. In accordance with his wishes I announced that his ashes would be scattered with those of Jonathan in the garden of remembrance. Robert's mother readily understood that as they had been together in life as friends, so they wished to be together in death. It is to her credit that, on her own initiative, she ensured that the two men were mentioned together in the crematorium's book of remembrance.

Jonathan may not have had a known mother in life but, through Robert, he had an adopted mother in death, a mother who retains contact with me.

Grieving for offspring

An expression in a letter from the mother of the first person I was involved with highlights the importance of Aids ministry, whoever is rendering it:

> I am sure it was through you that my dear son, in the last weeks, was able to be so calm and accept in faith what was happening to him, so thanks once again for all you did for him.
> It helped me such a lot, too.

In the normal course of life sons and daughters grieve for the loss of parents but the death of people as a result of Aids means that many parents grieve for their offspring.

However, a further outcome of Aids ministry is that in some instances it has been my privilege to conduct the funeral of a mother who has predeceased her son, thus reflecting involvement with families as a whole.

6.

Volunteering

THE United Kingdom is renowned for its voluntary organisations and individuals engaged in voluntary work. The Salvation Army is one such organisation.

As an officer, I have been commissioned and ordained according to the practices of the Army and am therefore regarded in law as a minister of religion. I've officiated at many marriages and have dedicated infants, as well as conducted all too many funerals. The Army's strength, however, lies in the multitude of volunteers worldwide who, coming from all walks of life, engage in its ministry of proclaiming the gospel and caring for the needy.

I shall ever be grateful, for example, for the many volunteers, as well as officers of The Salvation Army, who readily responded in time of need when I was National Emergency Officer dealing with disasters such as the Clapham Junction train crash, the Kegworth air disaster, and the Zeebrugge ferry catastrophe. It would be a sad day if governments ever ceased to appreciate their worth, or if volunteers became motivated by financial gain.

I have been moved by the generosity of people in time of need. For example, at the Clapham train crash where the Army had an emergency vehicle serving refreshments to firemen, police and ambulance crews, residents from nearby houses came out with platefuls of sandwiches. Colin Swan, driving a vehicle containing sandwiches, stopped and off-loaded them all for the Army to distribute. Boys from Emanuel School, adjacent to the railway, were allowed by Headmaster Peter Thompson to come and take trays of refreshments provided by the Army's team and distribute on site to those in need.

How welcome are people who generously give to voluntary organisations, such as the Army! Most voluntary organisations have limited resources to fall back on, but need regular funding for proper maintenance of their work and for special projects. Gift Aid and covenanted giving by people results in welcome additional income from the government.

Small voluntary organisations also have a vital role, such as the Chelsea & Westminster Hospital volunteers who undertook important work in the old St Stephen's Hospital, when there was need for much patient support in the Thomas Macaulay Ward, John Hunter Clinic and the newly built Kobler Centre.

In St Stephen's Hospital there was a very long corridor, with stairs at the end leading up to the Frontliners' Office – another small voluntary organisation of people upfront about their Aids diagnosis. These stairs also led to the John Hunter Clinic, where people came for counselling; testing for HIV, treatment and support.

On one side of the long corridor was the catering department and on the opposite side Alan ran the volunteers' office. Alan, assisted by other volunteers, arranged for the transport of patients, some of whom were very ill and weak; provided refreshments on the ward; did little extras for patients, such as buying newspapers etc, from local shops. All this gave support to the hard-working medical staff. Patients noticed the difference if per chance they were accommodated in other wards where volunteers were lacking!

In the past, local students have given a helping hand. Police cadets Jane Pack, Steve Ball, Iain Harkes and others joined the volunteers as part of their community service training. They were a great asset!

Writing in *STEVIES*, the newsletter of the St Stephen's Hospital Voluntary Services Department, Alan states:

> Many of you will be pleased to know that I have told my parents and family what they needed to know. Many thanks for the personal support that many of you gave me. It was a lot more difficult than I had anticipated. The 'perfect time' never happened and in the end I just told my poor mother in my normal blunt fashion. It wasn't easy, but it had to be done. After my friend Peter's death, I realised that parents have a right to know if one of their offspring is likely to pre-decease them. My parents have come to terms with the facts very sensibly and I feel that a weight has been lifted off my shoulders. I no longer have to pretend or deceive them any more. If I am ill or even admitted, they can know about everything.

Dear Alan was such a lovely person; we held him in high respect and affection and when he did, as feared, pre-decease his parents, we all missed him a lot. The money raised in lieu of flowers at his funeral resulted in a substantial sum for Mildmay Mission Hospital.

All past and present volunteers have had a crucial role in being supportive of patients, friends and relations, and medical staff. Mrs Jean Hunt is worthy of a national award. She is a veritable 'Mother in Israel' who became a volunteer in the mid-eighties. Her sandwiches and cakes and, above all, her pavlovas are renowned. Jean has enjoyed a tremendous sense of satisfaction and fulfilment in her unique ministry among patients, often joined by her husband, Tony, who has readily given a hand. At St Stephen's Hospital, and also when the ward was moved temporarily to the Westminster Hospital, in addition to the regular trolley service morning and afternoon providing tea, sandwiches and cakes, there was a Tuesday and Thursday afternoon teaparty. Those were great times, when patients who were able gathered in the large day room, joined by their loved ones, to share in fellowship and refreshments – including pavlova!

Nursing staff also popped in, if time permitted. It fostered good relationships between medical staff, volunteers, patients and their friends and relations.

Volunteers can often empathize with loved ones, enabling them to converse about patients and their own anxieties. This in itself is supportive of the nursing staff.

When I took General Eva Burrows out for the afternoon visiting people with Aids in February 1990, a visit to Westminster Hospital was included. As we entered the day room for the teaparty, Jean kindly took the General in hand, introduced her to all the patients by name, and included their friends and relations. This gesture was moving in itself, but I was all the more moved by the fact that Jean divulged to the General that her own son was HIV positive. Despite that heartache, Jean continued her ministry as a volunteer, an example to us all. No fame or glory attached to this activity but how dear to the heart of God it must be. Jean is just one example of the many, many unsung heroes out there in the community.

Simon, another volunteer, eventually took over Alan's responsibilities. He lived with his friend, Kevin, who had been interviewed on Central Television about his HIV status. Both gave valiant service as volunteers, despite periods of ill health. They always welcomed me into their home, hospital office or ward. All too soon, Father Bill Kirkpatrick was to conduct Kevin's funeral service in St Cuthbert's Church. I was glad to pay tribute to this fine young man. Later, when Simon died in 1995, his funeral in Our Lady of Dolours, the Servite Catholic Church in Fulham Road, was led by Father Philip Allen OSM with Father Bill Kirkpatrick, an Anglican, and me, a Salvationist, taking part. Ecumenics in action! Simon and Kevin left a legacy of committed volunteering that others have continued.

A glance at the National Aids Manual publication *UK Aids Directory* (ISBN 1898397090) indicates that there are a multitude of voluntary organisations, with few paid staff and many volunteers, and I have personally been grateful for the support of many of them.

It was always a pleasure to visit the Body Positive drop-in centre in Philbeach Gardens, Earls Court, to enjoy fellowship, refreshments and mutual support, their annual services in St Cuthbert's Church being one of the highlights of the year for so many people.

CARA was frequently resorted to when it was opposite London Lighthouse and there, too, Christian support was mutually beneficial.

A three-day workshop known as The Aids Mastery, organised by the Northern Lights Trust and held in River House, Hammersmith, was a unique opportunity to associate with 30 other people from different parts of the country and to extend one's knowledge. Jon and also Michael had urged me to apply for the course and I was glad I did so, not least because I met some great people.

I shall ever be indebted to Charlotte Platman and her colleagues at The Globe Centre for their support, not least in regard to my role in the lives of John and also Robert. I often had cause to think of how William Booth commenced what became The Salvation Army within a stone's throw of that centre in Mile End Road.

The pioneering organisation Frontliners brings back a lot of happy memories of my close association with members in the St Stephen's Hospital office and then their premises in Fulham Road, plus the office in Mildmay Mission Hospital, mentioned elsewhere in this volume.

Other organisations could also be mentioned, including those associated with my colleague Marjory Parrott, all of them having a crucial role in responding to the Aids pandemic. The Children With Aids Charity (CWAC), Aids Care Education & Training (ACET), CRUSAID, The Catholic Aids Link – all these and many more have their place within the United Kingdom.

Some have now ceased to exist, having served their purpose.

7.

Finance, Food, Furniture and Fashion

I T'S to the credit of people in charge of Salvation Army finances that they've been fully supportive of my ministry and only rarely has expenditure been queried.

Care in the use of limited resources breeds trust.

Finance

In the 1980s and early 1990s, people were often seriously ill or dying before their much-needed state benefits had been negotiated. Dealing with people's material requirements became a matter of urgency. In addition to my own awareness of the needs of individuals and families, social workers would submit applications to assist people, often women and children from ethnic minorities who needed household items or clothing.

Some HIV positive people had difficulty financing themselves for a number of reasons. Many were young professionals no longer earning good wages. Therefore they could not maintain a lifestyle to which they were accustomed. Acute sickness and diarrhoea, often with severe night sweats, frequently resulted in soiled bedding and clothing. Washing machines were constantly used, resulting in additional expenditure. Digestion problems and weight loss resulted in the need for good nutritious food, much of it costing more than they could afford on limited state income.

Food

End-of-day produce from Marks & Spencer was at times donated to the Army and, when suitable, colleagues would let me have fruit and other produce for the benefit of patients at home and in hospital. When state benefits were not so promptly given as now, some patients in their homes found it a struggle financially, so I was able to make up food

40-42 Trinity Road, Tooting Bec, SW17 (020 8767 7555)

parcels. This not only gave practical help but also much needed nutritious food, particularly as weight loss was an acute and common problem. For understandable reasons, Marks & Spencer rules governing food distribution are now much tighter, so in recent years I have no longer had this resource.

If non-perishable food became available, it would be put aside in order to make up food parcels for distribution to men and women and families during the Christmas period. In addition, a sufficient number of tins of biscuits were purchased for people with whom I was directly involved, mindful of the fact that a cuppa and a biscuit for a visitor is a bonus in what for some could be a lonely life when ill and at home.

In the early years of the pandemic, it was common to see and hear pillbox timers. These were little plastic containers, about the size of a box of Swan matches, into which people with HIV and Aids could put a limited number of pills.

The boxes would bleep at certain times to remind people to take their pills – rather confusing if a number of people with pillboxes were together and a bleep sounded, each person wondering if it was theirs. Again, for people in need, I was able to purchase a number of pillboxes from a store in the Kings Road, Chelsea, and thus help them to control their medication.

Furniture

Often there was need to rehouse people or improve their furnishings. In those days, the Army had a warehouse for secondhand furniture in Spa Road, Bermondsey, where the officers in charge generously helped in time of need. Either I would collect items, thankful for the use of a Ford Escort van, or it was sufficient for a social worker or client to take a letter from me to the officer in charge and for them to negotiate transport.

When the Wandsworth Oasis Aids Support Centre established the Wandsworth Oasis Trading Company Limited which, through its charity shops raises money to support people affected by Aids, it became another valued resource. When someone died and I was given responsibility for disposing of their furniture, some of it would be channelled to Oasis and the management in turn would help when I required furnishings for people in need. 'Wheeling and dealing', or rather begging and borrowing came to be something of a feature in those early years!

Fashion

Clothing, too, was an important issue. Many people with weight loss found clothes no longer fitted properly and they would feel the cold. For fashion-conscious young men and women this was an additional blow. I was thankful for clothing donated by such companies as C&A, not least because it boosted people's morale to have some new clothing that fitted them properly, was contemporary, and enabled them to keep warm.

'Hi, Trevor, can you help me?' called big John from across the Body Positive room in Earls Court. His height was matched by the size of his feet! He was in desperate need of new boots. Careful discussion resulted in the purchase of a pair of Dr Martens boots and the continued support of both big John and a close friend of his, another John. I will never forget the day when John lifted the frail figure of his friend in his strong arms and brought him to my car for the last trip to hospital. That friend, who had such a lovely personality, gave me a furry little white seal with big black eyes that is now perched on my television set, a pleasing reminder of him. These two good friends died within a year of each other. Despite her failing eyesight, John's mother in Ireland has continued to keep in contact.

The crucial issues of finance, food, furniture and fashion are not quite so acute as years ago but there are still needs to be met. I am eternally grateful for businesses and individuals that have confidence in the Army's ability to act justly and with mercy in time of need.

8.

Early Literature

THERE is a difference between the medical work of doctors/nurses and the spiritual ministry undertaken by ministers of religion and other people of faith. Yet both are engaged in the healing art, in a holistic sense, and at times the boundaries become blurred. I have worked alongside many excellent men and women nurses, who have been in holy orders. As nurses, they have done their work professionally, mostly without people being aware they are in holy orders, yet their faith has been their motivation and has enhanced their vocation as nurses.

A variety of books by people in medical and pastoral ministries have influenced my Aids ministry, especially in the early years of the pandemic.

Aids: A Catholic Call for Compassion, published in 1985 by Sheed & Ward of America, ISBN 0934134731 was the first.
The author, Eileen P. Flynn, was Assistant Professor at St Peter's College, Jersey City, where she taught medical ethics.

The Samaritan's Imperative: Compassionate Ministry to People Living with Aids, by Michael J. Christensen was published in 1991 by Abingdon Press, Nashville, ISBN 0687367905
An elder in the Church of the Nazarene, Michael was a chaplain in the Aids unit at San Francisco General Hospital.

Morning Glory Babies – Children with Aids and the Celebration of Life, by Tolbert McCarroll makes moving reading. Published in 1988 by Triangle/ SPCK, ISBN 0281044139.
It relates how the Starcross Community, a lay Catholic religious organisation, cared for orphaned babies with HIV/Aids in California. It is the story of commitment to care, despite initial opposition from people in the area, and conveys a message of hope.

As the author states:

> 'More than ever we recognised that the ultimate right of any child is not to die among strangers.'

The Army's own publications have had some impact, particularly outside the Army. As mentioned earlier (page 7) *Aids Care – Practical & Pastoral Guidelines*, published in 1987, ISBN 085412537X, had a print run of 10,000 copies and soon sold out. Though some of the language and advice sounds dated, much of it is still relevant.

The chapter concerning HIV- positive children in playgroups and schools is specially poignant.

At that time, Mildmay Mission Hospital commenced respite and terminal care of people with Aids. An article in *Capital Gay* dated 4 September 1987 gave rise to the front page headlines:

WRATH OF GOD EVANGELISTS TO OPEN AIDS HOSPICE
– THE BAD SAMARITANS

Thankfully, the hospital soon justified itself in practice and merited the plaudits of the same newspaper. Nevertheless it made me anxious about the Army's new publication.

Feeling like Daniel in the lions' den, in November 1987 I went to the offices of *Capital Gay*. Much to my relief, I was warmly received by the editor, Graham McKerrow, and by all his colleagues on the staff. Having explained the principles by which the Army was undertaking its worldwide ministry to people with Aids, the result was a brief but positive article. Obviously the article was read, as a number of people came to express appreciation of what the Army was doing.

This was followed by two Scriptographic publications, first issued for the American market but then 'Anglicised' for use in the United Kingdom. *A Christian Response to Aids* and *About Caring for People with Aids* both soon sold out.

COMMUNITY COUNSELLING

A handbook for facilitating care and change

Part of an integrated response
to
HIV and AIDS
by
The Salvation Army

FINDING HOPE IN
THE RIVER OF LIFE

A company which undertook many of the funerals I conducted, the West London funeral directors J. H. Kenyon, generously sponsored the publication of 10,000 copies of *Before and After – Advance Planning for Death and Funeral Arrangements*, a few copies of which remain in stock at Salvation Army headquarters – ISBN 0854126260.

They are also available via the charity shops of the Wandsworth Oasis Trading Co Ltd.

A handbook, *Community Counselling – Finding Hope in the River of Life* was produced by The Salvation Army International Headquarters in 1997. Though primarily designed for use in developing countries, this excellent manual contains insights, points for discussion, role plays and helpful methods of approach to HIV/Aids which could prove useful in many situations.

Mildmay Mission Hospital has given birth to several excellent books.

Palliative Care for People with Aids, by Ruth Sims and Veronica Moss, published by Edward Arnold – ISBN 0340613718, now in a second edition.

A Place of Growth: Counselling and Pastoral Care of People with Aids, by Alvin Marcetti and Shirley Lunn, published by Darton, Longman & Todd Ltd – ISBN 0232520259.

A Time to Care: Mildmay Hospital's Response to People with Aids, by Ruth Sims, with foreword by Diana, Princess of Wales, published by Hodder & Stoughton Ltd – ISBN 0340661488.

Aids: A Strategy for Nursing Care, by Robert J. Pratt, published in 1988 by Edward Arnold – ISBN 0713145757, is a must for anyone engaged in nursing people with Aids.

Father Bill Kirkpatrick's books are helpful to people in pastoral ministry. They include:

*Going Forth: A Practical and Spiritual Approach
   to Dying and Death,*   ISBN 0232522375
Aids: Sharing the Pain – Pastoral Guidelines,   ISBN 0232517487
Cry Love, Cry Hope – Responding to Aids,   ISBN 0232520704

This last includes chapters by many people, myself included. All are published by Darton, Longman & Todd.

In his book *Living on the Edge – An Experience of Aids*, published by Marshall Pickering, ISBN 0551027495, Michael Kelly speaks from experience, born of an optimistic spirit. Just as he was industrious in business, he was likewise when he had Aids, initiating a fund-raising venture to raise £35,000 for a new lift at Mildmay Mission Hospital. National newspapers featured him meeting Diana, Princess of Wales, in Mildmay, where he appreciated skilled nursing care. Speaking of one of his experiences, Michael relates:

> Soon after the burglary, I had signed up my contents with The Salvation Army General Insurance Corporation. Following a further burglary, when his home was ransacked, he writes: I thanked God I was insured this time. At least it would soften the blow financially. I sent off a claim form backed up by a police report the next day, and within four days a cheque from The Salvation Army for the correct amount plopped through my front door. I cannot recommend them highly enough.

Many other books could be recommended but those are a taster of what has been available.

Video

Videos, too, have had their place. I particularly commend those produced by CWAC – Children With Aids Charity at Lion House, 3 Plough Yard, London EC2A 3LP, fax 020 7247 9115. The actors featured are young people who have an excellent way of presenting the subject in such videos as *Problem?* and *HIV Risky Business*.

In the 1980s I was particularly grateful for the mutual support of Marcus Stephan, Development Officer at the British Red Cross Society National Headquarters, where it was a pleasure to meet him and his colleagues. This link with Marcus continued through the years. The society and the Health Education Authority eventually issued a video on HIV/Aids Education for Seafarers that has been useful when speaking of the subject with staff at Army hostels.

Language

Language, particularly in the early years, was a crucial issue in Aids ministry. It was so easy to fall into the trap of using negative language, words that put people down instead of raising them up – victim; a person suffering from Aids, etc. The 30 May 1987 edition of *The War Cry* featured the subject of Aids in a full back page article headed 'Aids Victim Beats Despair', in which I relate the story of a fellow for whom I cared. Quite an achievement to have such an article in those early years when fear, ignorance and hostility was rampant, even though I was unhappy with the editor's headline.

I ventured to engage with editorial colleagues in discussion about language when addressing the subject of Aids. To their credit they were positive rather than negative in their response. 'A person living with Aids' is preferable to 'A person dying of Aids' as it implies they are able to assert themselves, able to take control of their lives. The first phrase offers hope, the latter speaks of doom. 'A person with Aids', or PWA, became common parlance, rather than the negative sounding 'Victim of Aids'.

Even when dealing with a subject as emotive as rape, language is equally important. 'Victim' smacks of helplessness, whereas 'A person who has been raped' conveys a more positive image.

And at the other end of the scale, even the phrase 'those people' can be stated in a derogatory manner, as if we are superior to them, smacking of self-righteousness.

Colleagues engaged in the Army's editorial and publishing work have throughout the years supported my ministry. By means of articles written or initiated by me and other people, they have continually raised the profile of the subject of Aids, helping to keep people informed and alert to the dangers of the pandemic in the midst of society.

I have had much discussion with them about whether to print AIDS or Aids – a point that to this day continues to be debated in other circles. Suffice to say the Army usually follows the style of *The Times* and uses 'Aids'.

Mind you, it did once cause me a problem. Years ago, I was invited to address an over-60 club meeting on the subject of Aids but to our mutual embarrassment they thought I was going to speak about wheelchairs and other forms of assistance for the elderly.

Which leads nicely into the next chapter!

9.

Laughter

DENNIS was highly respected and competent in his profession. He was popular with colleagues and enjoyed his work. It was a pleasure to associate with him and his flatmate. Noreen, a competent nurse, was a good friend of his, someone he felt able to telephone in time of need, or with a view to a cuppa and meal together. Sadly, the time came when Dennis became very ill and was accommodated in a side room of the ward. A pleasant room, with an armchair, generous floor space, a good outlook from the window, and a picture of dolphins on the wall. He had plenty of visitors, including many workplace colleagues.

It came to the stage when for three nights I stayed with him in the room, dozing in the armchair or lying on a mattress on the floor, wakeful for his every need. I recalled my years as a medic in the Royal Air Force, sleeping but alert to any sound and responsive to telephone calls or buzzing bells. I would rise early and, bleary eyed and dishevilled, shuffle to the bathroom, hopeful that the nurses did not think too ill of me. On leaving the hospital I felt like screaming to the world, 'Don't you realise what's happening here? A life is ebbing away and you are blithely going about your workaday activities.' Then the world of normality would embrace me and, with an aching heart, I would set about my daily tasks.

One Sunday I was due to conduct morning and evening services at Chalk Farm, where the officer, Bill Cochrane, was off ill. Being free in the afternoon I decided to return to hospital to be with Dennis. A nurse remarked, 'Trevor, you daren't leave Dennis now, he's unlikely to last the day.' What was I to do? Where was my priority? Was I to be like the priest in the parable of the Good Samaritan, to 'pass by on the other side' and hurry to my religious duties? I phoned Bill, who kindly arranged for last-minute leadership of the evening service. Letting the congregation down at such short notice caused me much embarrassment.

41

I was all the more embarrassed when, later, I had to relate that Dennis survived for a further three weeks! A number of us would gather of an evening in Dennis's room. Yes, we were distressed for him. But those evening gatherings were sometimes hilarious and a tonic for us all, particularly for Dennis. If we fancied a McDonalds I would hurry to the shop in Victoria and bring a pile back for the group. Raucous laughter could be heard until late in the evening. Well, why not? Humour was very much part of Dennis's life and was better than 'doom and gloom' visitations.

Dennis was 'hedging his bets' in regard to religion. I was there as a friend, and represented the Army. Anglican Father Bill Kirkpatrick also came on regular visits. Staff Nurse Pearl Lenihan who was giving him superb care was in holy orders, and had attached a small statuette of the Virgin Mary to the head of the bed with Sellotape. Hospital chaplain, the Reverend Bernard Hughes, joined us one evening and brought his own ministry. If, with all these means of interdenominational intercession with the Almighty, Dennis didn't enter Heaven then I'll want to know why! Joking aside, I am sure our concern for Dennis was but a dim reflection of the Almighty's concern for his spiritual wellbeing.

One weekend, Dennis's friend Noreen was visiting her sister in Wales and I was conducting Sunday services at Llanelli. Just as I was about to walk to the rostrum to lead the service, a telephone call was received intimating that Dennis had died. Few would have realised how I felt when conducting the services. Though hearts were breaking, Noreen and I later laughed at the possibility that Dennis must have thought in typical humorous style he would get one over on us by departing this life when neither of us were with him, but far away in Wales. Trust Dennis!

Father Bill conducted the funeral service in London, with those of us who were friends participating. Some days later, Noreen and I journeyed to Yorkshire where, in the presence of the family, I interred Dennis's ashes in the family grave. As Noreen and I dealt with his estate, there was a natural sense of sadness but it was tempered by laughter.

It was as Dennis would have wished.

Humour has in so many instances been a positive ingredient of Aids ministry. If there is also the ability to laugh at one's self, so much the better! Reading between the lines of Scripture I sense that our Lord himself was blessed with a good sense of humour.

I've certainly needed one to lighten the load of my Aids ministry.

10.

A Lasting Image

WHEN responsible for Salvation Army youth work in the Eastern Counties from 1967 to 1971, I was glad of association with Ian, son of Fintain and Margaret Deoheney of Thetford. A lively, 17 year-old member of the Army, he readily joined the groups of young men and women who occasionally came to my house for discussion and prayer – and an abundance of food! Well, there had to be a reason for the visits! Ian's passion was to own a motorbike. His father agreed on condition that he took driving lessons. When going for his last lesson, Ian was hit head-on by a lorry and instantly killed. I shared with everyone, particularly his parents, the intense sense of shock and grief that found expression in his funeral service that I conducted. His parents have continued to maintain contact through the years.

To add to the heartbreak, they had no good, up-to-date photograph of Ian – just a snapshot taken as a child. I have had that in mind when ministering to people with Aids, particularly in the early years of the pandemic, for here we have predominantly young men and women dying before their parents and sometimes there have been no good photographs with which to remember them.

Around the time of Ian's accident, we were staging the Salvation Army musicals *Take-over Bid* and *Hosea*. They were great times of fellowship that included association with the Bryant family of Beccles. Robin Bryant later became the Army's official photographer, having his own studio at headquarters.

Years later, when Aids was taking its toll of human life, I had in mind my experience in the Eastern Counties and the lack of a good photograph of Ian. Mindful of the need for people to have good portrait photographs taken before, perhaps, health declines and the possibility of a photograph is shunned, I have suggested that Robin would take photographs. As a result, he has readily responded whenever I have brought someone to his studio. It has been another means of introducing people to the Army! It has given me real joy to see Robin's achievements through the years and I have been grateful for his support in many ways.

Another factor is that it helps to have a photograph on the front page of the order of service for funerals. It makes the order of service more personal and appreciated, particularly when people take it away, ponder the photo and have time to absorb the contents of the service, which I like to have typed in full – Bible readings and prayers included.

I sometimes use my photograph albums as an aid to prayer, placing them before me and turning the pages, remembering each individual as I visualize them and their partners, families and friends.

Try the tactic.

It's what they call intercessory prayer.

Lasting Images for relatives and friends

Pierre - see page 108

David - see pages 113-4

David - see page 125

Who should I be praying for

?

44

11.

Hospital Chapels

DESPITE strident calls from some quarters for a secularist society, I believe there is increasing recognition of the need for a holistic approach to people's wellbeing. By that I mean acknowledging and responding to the needs of the whole person – body, mind and spirit. It might be a useful exercise for politicians of all parties to indicate their policies under each heading! We might then work for an even better society.

Most hospitals make some provision for people's spiritual needs. Not only through much needed hospital chaplains and visiting ministers but also by providing hospital chapels and, sometimes, quiet rooms.

I would recommend anyone visiting a loved one in hospital, to suss out the hospital chapel and make time to go there, even for just a few minutes. Whether religious or not, it is refreshing to go into a place of comparative quietness and, usually, beauty. It can be calming to the mind and spirit. Pray if you wish but, if not, then just sit quietly, imbibe the quietness and let some degree of inner tranquility embrace heart and mind.

If concerned for someone I'm visiting, I go into the chapel to pray. When words are hard to find, I remember Paul's teaching:

> The Holy Spirit helps us in our distress. For we don't even know what we should pray for, nor how we should pray. But the Holy Spirit prays for us with groanings that cannot be expressed in words.
>
> (Romans 8:26, *NLT*)

In effect, God the Spirit fathoms our innermost being and interprets the longings of our hearts. So I just sit quietly and let the Spirit speak.

Hospital chapels vary in style. In London, St Bartholomew's Hospital chapel evinces an air of quiet calm and a sense of history; the Middlesex is exotic with beautiful mosaics; Charing Cross has beauty in its simplicity; the modern Chelsea & Westminster chapel has a blend of the old and the new, while the modest Mildmay Mission Hospital chapel is a place of frequent resort.

Whatever their character, each is a place where quietness is offered, the human spirit uplifted, the heart comforted and hope is increased.

Chris approached me hesitantly . . . 'Trevor, a number of us who know you wonder if you would visit a friend of ours. He's terminally ill. He's an atheist, doesn't believe in God, but would like to see you and plan for you to conduct his funeral.' At times we have to work within the limits of a person's understanding. Here was a young man, near to the end, wanting to trust someone he had not met but had heard of from friends. It would not have been appropriate to bash him on the head with the Bible! In any case, I prefer to adopt other tactics!

On the ward I found him breathing heavily through an oxygen mask, plainly terminally ill. But there was no other barrier between us and we conversed with ease. No, he had no belief in God but he did believe in 'the spiritual dimension of life.' So we worked within these limits. Older people find it difficult enough to prepare their wills, let alone their funeral services, yet here was a young man realistically facing the future and being considerate towards his friends. Having respect for this man's beliefs – or lack of them – and also mindful of those who would attend his funeral, some of whom would have a personal faith, a draft order of service was prepared.

Even people of no faith rarely object to such Bible readings as Ecclesiastes 3 or 1 Corinthians 13. Other readings and music together with my own oration would embrace everyone present. On such occasions it is like coming to a table laden with good things, and I invite people to take just what is right for them.

That fine young man was not seen again in this life, as all too soon I conducted his funeral. He exhibited calm courage as he faced death. In acknowledging the 'spiritual dimension' he touched a nerve of the soul and I am confident our Heavenly Father has embraced him with loving understanding.

No funeral service I've conducted has been secular, devoid of religious content. Everyone wanting me to conduct a funeral has been aware that I'm an officer of The Salvation Army and therefore will conduct a service from a Christian standpoint, yet that I will also have respect for those of no faith, those searching for faith, and those of other faiths. Whether in hospital chapel or elsewhere, there is the need to acknowledge the 'spiritual dimension' of life. In the hospital chapel, a simple moment of quietness, of prayer or contemplation, can do much to enhance one's spiritual wellbeing.

12.

Respect and Affection

DURING the height of the Troubles in Northern Ireland in the early seventies, I was responsible for Salvation Army youth work throughout Ireland. In the course of giving pastoral care to people at times of bombing or shooting incidents and street riots, I learned to

> Rejoice with them that do rejoice, and weep with them that weep
> (Romans 12:15, *KJV*).

The final incident I attended was when two young girls, playing beside their Hallowe'en bonfire on a street in the docklands area of Belfast, were killed by a car bomb which went off alongside Benny's Bar. Eleven other people were injured. Assisted by colleagues, hot drinks and food were distributed to factory and shop keepers, whose premises had been wrecked, and to police, firemen and servicemen to stem the coldness of the autumn night. I was readily received into people's devastated homes, seeking to minister to the residents, an action for which Roman Catholic priests expressed appreciation next day.

This enhanced sensitivity to people in need proved an asset when engaging in the Aids ministry. However, I have to admit that there still are times when I am insensitive!

I have never had so many hugs and kisses in my life as in ministry to people affected by Aids. Why should footballers have it all their own way! Patients and nurses, friends and relations, have all engaged in such acts of recognition, affection and appreciation. And I'm not complaining! It has all been so very natural, a reflection of the shared concern for each other and recognition of the fact that I am welcome as both minister and friend, someone caught up in the joys and sorrows that beset us.

If such actions smacked of falseness, had an element of showmanship, or were demeaning, I would not respond. I would not allow them to undermine my own integrity and the respect in which the Army is held. Such actions of familiarity must arise out of genuine trust, love and respect. I guess the same considerations apply when engaging in 'The Peace' in worship, when we greet each other with a handshake and sometimes a hug. There is a risk of pretentiousness!

If on entering the Thomas Macaulay Ward Nurse Noreen O'Donoghue gives me a hug, it not only reflects friendship but also the sometimes harrowing experiences we have shared, particularly in the earlier years of the Aids pandemic.

If on entering the crowded Kobler Centre, where people receive outpatient treatment, a fellow jumps up and gives me a hug, it is recognition of friendship, and, more often than not, of shared bereavement experiences. Chris came to me in London Lighthouse after I had conducted yet another funeral in the Ian McKellen Hall and, giving me a big hug, exclaimed, 'Oh Trevor, how many more?' That heart-breaking cry, wrenched from the depths of his being, carried an echo in my own heart and mind, not least because his own demise was not far distant.

Initially taken aback by such familiarity, I soon came to value its worth, so often conveying what words cannot express. To conduct a funeral and then give a loved one a hug is sometimes sufficient for that moment, an endorsement of all that has been said and done in the service. Words can wait.

And to be honest there have been times when I, too, have needed a hug as I have walked this sometimes lonely path. As they say in Scotland, where I enjoyed living for some years, 'Some things are better felt than telt.'

But hugs and kisses also reflect times of celebration. How good to join a large crowd of doctors and nurses and a few close friends in a celebratory meal to mark the retirement of Pearl Lenihan. A skilled nurse, who is also a sister in religious life, Pearl's co-operation through the years has been personally appreciated, her TLC extending beyond the patients to include the likes of me.

Exercise in the gym is good for the body and the mind. Perhaps hugging has a place, too. Here's a reading from an unknown author :

Hugging is healthy. It helps the body's immunity system. It keeps you healthy. It cures depression. It reduces stress. It induces sleep. It is invigorating. It is rejuvenating. It has no unpleasant side effects and hugging is nothing less than a miracle drug.

Hugging is all natural. It is organic and naturally sweet. No pesticides, no preservatives, no artificial ingredients and one hundred percent wholesome.

Hugging is practically perfect. There are no movable parts. No batteries to wear out. No periodic check-ups. Low energy consumption. High energy yield. Inflation proof. Non-fattening. No monthly payments. No insurance requirements. Theft-proof. Non-taxable. Non-polluting and, of course, fully returnable.

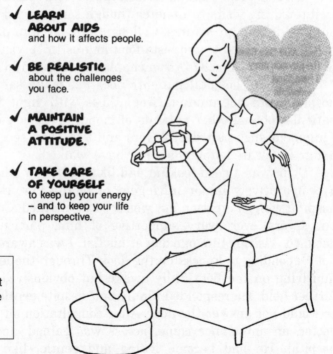

So--

GIVING CARE TO A PERSON WITH AIDS IS A GIFT OF LOVE!

✓ **LEARN ABOUT AIDS** and how it affects people.

✓ **BE REALISTIC** about the challenges you face.

✓ **MAINTAIN A POSITIVE ATTITUDE.**

✓ **TAKE CARE OF YOURSELF** to keep up your energy – and to keep your life in perspective.

Inside back cover of Scriptographic pamphlet About Caring for People with Aids see page 37

Your loving care makes a difference!

13.

Family Tracing Service
and Prison Ministries

WANDSWORTH, Brixton, Wormwood Scrubs and Belmarsh Prisons are familiar places to me for, as in society at large, some people with Aids break the law and end up in prison, including a few of those to whom I have ministered. Visits have been appreciated, particularly if there is little or no contact with family and there may be few friends. The Army's prison ministries personnel have usually facilitated my visits to inmates though sometimes I have gone through normal visiting procedures. Colleagues involved in prison ministry have readily responded to requests for inmates to be visited. Currently, The Salvation Army has 87 prison chaplains visiting 106 prisons.

Becoming hospital patients does not make saints of people! Even hospitals are not immune from those with 'light fingers', visitors or patients robbing other patients of money or other possessions. Hospital equipment such as video players and television sets in day rooms have had to be secured otherwise they have 'walked'.

Colin was a good-looking and likeable fellow who, sadly, committed a comparatively minor infringement of the law. He ended up in the hospital wing of a prison but was soon discharged. Colin had few friends but several were very supportive of him, particularly when health declined. Visiting him one day at his flat, I was aware that he was in but not responding to knocks on the door. Through the letterbox, I could see him lying on the floor, fully awake but obviously dementia had taken further hold. He responded kindly but, despite gentle urgings, could not or would not answer the door. After consultation on the phone with his doctor, an ambulance came, access was gained, and he was taken to hospital. He had become loving and gentle, like a child, so when discharged from hospital one of his friends decided to temporarily live with him, giving him tender loving care, aided by others of us.

50

Thankfully, he had made his will prior to becoming very ill, so as executor I knew precisely what he wanted done, ably supported by his friends.

The Army's Family Tracing Service has always been supportive and worked to our mutual benefit. The combination of the Prison Ministries, the Family Tracing Service and my own ministry, is evident in the story of John, first published in *The War Cry* in January 1991, which I quote with slight adaptation:

John's patience had finally snapped. His nerves were on edge, and a fellow resident at the hostel had been getting on to him. So, in a fit of rage, he hit the man on the head. The wound needed stitches, and the attack – although provoked – resulted in John being brought before the magistrate.

John was HIV positive, and he recalled, 'I was handcuffed and kept on my own in the coach, which I thought was out of order and hostile. When we stopped at Pucklechurch Prison, everyone went into lunch except yours truly. I couldn't work it out, so I put it down to ignorance and bad attitude. We eventually reached the Moor, in all the smog, and I didn't like the look of the place one bit. We all went to reception, where I was taken through first and whisked off to the hospital cell. I was banged up 23 hours a day. I've done 21 months in prison hospital.'

In spite of problems, John received care and support from many prison officers. The companionship of another inmate, whom he met briefly during slopping out, was important to him in those days. During this period, in addition to attending prison chapel, John was baptised. His testimony, encouragement and example had a profound impact for good on other inmates and staff.

John knew he was developing Aids, so asked the Salvation Army prison visitor, George Hardy, if the Family Tracing Service would locate his mother. He had had no contact with her since he and his brother had been taken into local authority care when he was five. He was overjoyed to receive word that his mother, stepfather and brother had been traced.

When John's health deteriorated he was released on parole to the Royal Naval Hospital in Plymouth for several weeks. Accompanied by another person on parole and a senior customs and excise officer, John was then taken to Westminster Hospital, London, to benefit from staff skilled in the care of people with Aids. At this hospital John was introduced to Trevor Smith on one of his regular visits. The visits continued, both at the Westminster Hospital and later when John became terminally ill and was transferred to Mildmay Mission Hospital. There John welcomed a visit by his mother and stepfather, and also his brother who by this time had been reunited with his parents and was living with them. Shortly afterwards, on returning to London following an appointment, Trevor Smith discovered that John had died. He visited the family and later conducted John's funeral. 'I won't be dictated to by a poxy virus!' John had once declared. But although the effects of that virus resulted in his death at the age of 30, John had come to experience much loving care from prison staff, inmates and other friends – including Salvation Army officers and hospital staff. Above all, being reunited with his family symbolised another fact – that John was also reunited with God. It was something he was glad to tell others about.

Having attended meetings of the All-Party Parliamentary Group on Aids, I was all the more glad to attend a joint meeting with the All-Party Parliamentary Group on Homelessness and Housing Need. Care of the homeless, including former inmates, and housing needs have been a pertinent aspect of Aids and in other spheres of ministry. It gave opportunity to raise an issue that was minuted.

I visited a young man with HIV, who possessed a lot of initiative. Having obtained a small flat, he furnished it with items off skips, even a microwave oven, plus items that others of us were able to supply. (I also visited a fellow in the Pimlico district, who likewise had furnished his flat with excellent items from skips. I hesitate to recommend this policy, as I believe it is illegal, but I do not blame the men.) He was a likeable person, as was the young lady he was getting to know.

Unfortunately a misdemeanour resulted in him spending a short time in prison, where I visited him. A vexed issue was that, as an inmate, he lost his modest housing association flat. In anticipation of his discharge, I was told that nothing could be lined up for him, that on discharge he must report to the local authority housing office and declare himself as homeless. The office would be under obligation to house him temporarily in a hotel or hostel, in the hope that he might eventually get permanent accommodation. Having HIV and possessed of a modest amount of money in his pocket and little of this world's goods, on discharge he was obviously a vulnerable young man.

I did not want him to jump the housing queue but it did annoy me that, having so recently had accommodation, nothing could be lined up prior to discharge. As it was, he was put into a rather poor hotel, where he had items stolen from him. Yet one more issue to consider when it comes to reducing factors that put pressure on former inmates to reoffend.

14.

An Oasis

IN THE 1980s there was a great deal of public ignorance and fear in regard to Aids. Misinformation and terms such as the 'gay plague' prejudiced the thinking of many people, feeding the fear. In the medical profession some people initially viewed the new pandemic with fear and extreme cautionary measures were taken.

A number of funeral directors refused to conduct the funerals of people with Aids, or adopted extreme steps to prevent infection. Even in the church some vocal people pronounced judgment and the 'wrath of God' upon those with Aids. One of the first funerals I conducted from Mildmay Mission Hospital occurred when I was asked to do it because another minister had refused.

There was an obvious need for places where people with Aids, their friends and relations, could go for relaxation, fellowship and refreshment; places where they could feel safe and away from hostile attitudes. As a result, centres were established in a number of towns and cities, particularly in London, some giving rise to well established organisations such as Body Positive.

In 1985 Richard Crowe was leader of the Army's work in Wandsworth, seeking to minister to people in the community as a whole. Having had contact with motorbike enthusiasts, he was requested to conduct the funeral of a biker who had died as a result of Aids. This increased his awareness of the dire threat of Aids in this country.

In co-operation with his own Army centre membership and the affected community, Richard organised a Christmas carol service on 17 December 1985, at which the Army's International Medical Adviser, Dr Paul du Plessis, addressed the subject of Aids and its prevention. The Mayor of Wandsworth, Councillor Maurice Heaster, graced the proceedings.

Many people attended, ranging from church representatives to prostitutes, not only to celebrate Christmas but also to educate themselves in regard to Aids. Money raised from the venture went to St George's Hospital to help develop its work for people with Aids. Further donations for the hospital arose – not least from more funerals that were conducted.

The subject of Aids was of particular concern to Patrick Lethaby, a business representative for Monument Tools Ltd, who travelled the world in connection with his work and who attended the Army, although at that time he was not a member.

Patrick engaged in discussion with Richard Crowe and pursued discussions in other ways, not least by writing to Paul du Plessis in April 1987. He proposed practical ways in which the Army in this country could become even more involved in ministry: involve more people in visitation of those with Aids; fund-raising for the support of people; increase ministry to friends and relations; assisting, when needed, in the clearing of people's homes following deaths.

In his letter, Patrick remarks:

> I have been talking to friends in pubs, clubs and other organisations on what help can be given. Many of them would like the Army to help because it's a popular and well-known and trusted organisation.

His concern, allied with that of others, resulted in a support centre being established at the Army in Wandsworth.

On 30 June 1989 the Wandsworth Oasis Aids Support Centre was officially launched. This was a venture promoted as a result of the co-operation between the affected community and the Army. Initially it entailed a drop-in at the Army on Saturdays between 10am and 5pm but this was later changed to afternoon and evening. Bob Freese ably supported Patrick by using his skill to produce a modest newsletter and to deal with other paperwork. The leader of the local Army at that time, Vivienne Wileman, gave the venture tremendous support, becoming its chaplain.

Theatre and other outings were arranged – even a guided tour behind the scenes at Mortlake Crematorium! The imminence of death was very real in those days, so such an outing brought a measure of reassurance about how the body is handled with respect following a funeral service. An annual 'Friends Remembering Friends' Service and carol service has continued to be held throughout the years and is still attracting many people.

The Wandsworth venture sparked the establishment of Oasis centres elsewhere. Gladys Thompson initiated the one attached to the Army's hostel in Belfast. That in Edinburgh was led by Mary Hutson, who later attended the Army's international conference on Aids, held in Switzerland. The one in Manchester by Jacqui Griffiths, who worked closely with the local hospital and community. At the Army in Cardiff Splott district, Robert Pearce, ably followed by his successors, plus colleagues and the affected community established another effective Oasis.

As far away as in South Africa, an Oasis was established by Bert and Nancy Roper, British Salvation Army Officers serving there at the time. Like the Wandworth Oasis, it was inspired by Patrick Lethaby, who had shared his vision with Bert and Nancy while on holiday in Johannesburg. The venture was successful, gaining the support of the theatrical community, which acknowledged the Army's pioneering response to the Aids pandemic.

A further outcome was support given to Dr Paul du Plessis in establishing Ethembeni – Zulu for 'Place of Hope' – as a place catering for babies and orphans with HIV/Aids.

The worth of the Oasis drop-in centres was real and effective, resulting in additional activities that included services of remembrance and funerals, plus social events. Speaking with appreciation at the Wandsorth Oasis carol service Michael, whose story is related elsewhere in this book, writes:

> Though I don't attend Oasis on a regular basis, I do feel very much part of Oasis. Over the years I have seen people cross your doors – often people without hope – resulting in them finding their way and finding within themselves the strength and courage to continue on their way. You have much for which to be proud. Your example has been a source of inspiration to others concerned about the Army's response to the Aids pandemic. I do hope that as time goes by you, the soldiers and adherents of Wandsworth Army and those who are members and friends of Oasis, will continue to give an innovative lead to activities within The Salvation Army. I feel confident enough to say you have been a pinpoint of light to others, just by welcoming and assuring people of God's welcoming acceptance.

Since those early years, a number of national and local drop-ins have come to a natural end including some Oasis centres. Those at Chalk Farm and Wandsworth have developed and gained their own independent charitable status but still work in co-operation with the Army. At Chalk Farm the work was first established by Brad of the affected community and the Army's local leader, Bill Cochrane. Brad, otherwise known as Dr Bradley J. S. Hepburn, a USA licensed vet, was studying and teaching at the Royal Veterinary College.

Local citizens, including Glenda Jackson MP, have been very supportive of the venture that now has a broad range of activities but maintains a drop-in. Recently, due to changes affecting the Army property, it changed its name to the North London Oasis and moved to the Kentish Town district but the Army's current local leader, James Williams, has continued to provide chaplaincy. Other members of the Army have been involved, including Robert, who as editor produced a highly commended newsletter, printed by Kall Kwik of the Elephant & Castle.

Wandsworth Oasis has ceased as a drop-in, but continues charitable work in a modest way. However, emerging from the original Wandsworth Oasis is an independent charity known as Wandsworth Oasis Trading Company Ltd. The work of the company has extended from a charity shop in Battersea Park Road to three other shops, the last being in Streatham.

Money raised by these shops helps individuals affected by Aids as well as centres such as the Mildmay Mission Hospital. In addition, Chalk Farm Oasis and CRUSAID, an independent fund-raising charity, as well as the Trading Company have helped fund respite care for a number of people affected by Aids. Occasionally, I have requested funding for such care for people.

Associated with Cardiff Oasis were David and Allan, who converted a farmhouse and established both their home and a respite care wing. Situated 18 miles from Swansea, in the Gower Peninsula, holidays at the farmhouse for people affected by Aids, were funded by Wandsworth Oasis and Chalk Farm Oasis, which gave me the chance to help some of those to whom I ministered.

At times when I have needed to dispose of bric-a-brac or furnishings that belonged to the deceased, Wandsworth Oasis Trading Company Ltd and the Chalk Farm charity shop have readily accepted such items. In return they have helped me with items when I have needed them for people with Aids.

Much else could be written about the value of these centres but I guess it is for others to relate, if they so wish, the full history.

15.

Poetry

THOUGH I am appreciative of excellent teachers I had when young, my introduction to poetry was repellant. To learn a poem by heart and recite it in front of the class, was a nightmare. Thankfully, particularly in Aids ministry, my appreciation of poetry has been enhanced. For some people poetry has been a means of expressing deep thoughts and emotions.

In 1987, a seminar entitled *Aids and the Carer* was convened by the Westminster Pastoral Foundation. It was led by Ann Horton SRN, Health Adviser at the John Hunter Clinic, and the Reverend Martin Hazel of the United Reformed Church.

We had read to us a passage entitled 'A life in the woods' from *Bambi* by Felix Salten (translated by Whittaker Chambers – ISBN 0899663583). Two leaves, deep in conversation, cling to the top of an oak tree in autumn. One is heard to say:

> 'So many of us have fallen off tonight, we're almost the only ones left'
>
> 'You never know who's going to go next,' said the other. 'Even when it was warm and the sun shone, a storm or cloudburst would come and many leaves were torn off, though they were still young . . .
>
> 'Can it be true,' said the first leaf, 'can it really be true that others come to take our places when we're gone and after them still others, and more and more? . . .'
>
> 'What happens to us when we have fallen?' said the other.
>
> The first leaf answered, 'I don't know, some say one thing, some another, but nobody knows'
>
> The second leaf asked, 'Do we feel anything, do we know anything about ourselves when we're down there?'
>
> 'Who knows? Not one of all those down there has ever come back to tell us about it'.

The conversation continued in similar vein until one of them was torn from her place and spun down – Winter had come.

Based on this story, we were invited to write a letter as from an autumn leaf to the tree from whence it came. The underlying theme reflects the Aids ministry in which I was involved and what I experienced in the early years of the pandemic, so I wrote:

The Falling Leaf

Dear Tree,

I didn't like to admit to our parting – and yet it came.
Too late to say all the things I would like to have said.
This letter is inadequate but,well, let me say thanks.
Thanks for the strength drawn from you.
Thanks for the high, the enlarged perspective of life
    you gave me.
I hope my dying will somehow enrich you,
    despite the trauma through which I'm going.
Remember me.
Remember
    how you took pride in my fresh, newborn green;
    the maturity of summer months;
    then the warm, red glow of autumn.
Remember
    how firmly you held me when the storms of life blew strong.
I give you in death what you gave me in life
    – life, nourishment, future.
Let not my dying be in vain,
    for in me lies your future,
    the lives of generations of leaves as yet unborn.
Let those who will,
    shove me in a plastic bag and destroy me as garbage;
    burn me as in a funeral pyre of the fallen;
    tread me under foot, as of no consequence.
I return to the earth from whence I came
    and in so doing will rise again.

Let Mother Earth welcome me into her warm embrace,
    that the loneliness of death may be assuaged.
So, Tree,
    thank you for life, for death and hope.
Your friend,

Leaf

Poetry

I have occasionally commissioned songs and poems, such as for the Army's 'Quest' week – an event for young adults, designed to promote spiritual growth. Catherine Baird, a veritable saint of the Army, wrote the following. Though not written with Aids ministry specifically in mind, I like to think that the spirit of the song is reflected by all of us engaged in ministry to people affected by Aids.

The Sacred Gift

Love is the gift of the Spirit,
    Treasure beyond all compare,
Sent from the heart of the Father,
    Talent most sacred and rare;
Though I grow daily in wisdom,
    Toiling new knowledge to prove,
These cannot succour the neighbour
    Jesus has bid me to love.

Into the ocean of Thine,
Into the ocean of Thine,
Pouring my talent for loving
Into the ocean of Thine.

How shall I love my Creator,
    Author and Giver of grace,
Love him with heart, mind and spirit
    When I have not seen His face?
Jesus, Thy cross is the answer,
    Weeping I witness Thy pain,
Through the dark hour of Thy suff'ring
    Death cannot threaten Thy reign.

Humbly I kneel, my Redeemer,
    Waiting and looking above,
Here, in the hour of Thy glory,
    Watching the triumph of love;
Small though the chalice I'm bringing,
    Offering all that is mine,
Pouring my talent for loving
    Into the ocean of Thine.

Catherine Baird
(Music by Peter Ayling, *Musical Salvationist* July 1982, SP&S Ltd)

Mindful of Aids ministry, Mona Westergaard responded to my challenge and wrote a poem based on our Lord's words:

Verily I say unto you, inasmuch as ye have done it unto one of the least of these my brethren, ye have done it unto me

(Matthew 25:40, KJV).

Gospel of 'The Inasmuch'

God of 'The Inasmuch',
Lord of the healing touch,
   Your way we take.
Help us to serve our kind,
Lost souls to seek and find,
The broken heart to bind
   For Jesus' sake.

God of the poor and weak,
Refuge of those who seek,
   Give us we pray
A caring love for all,
Patience with those who fall,
Resolve that meets the call
   Of our today.

God of the proud and strong
Who cover grief with song
   That none may guess
The hurt that in them lies,
Grant us discerning eyes
To see and sympathize
   With their distress.

God of forgiving love,
Saviour who died to prove
   Redemption's case,
Use us the cross to bear,
Let us your purpose share
Salvation to declare
   In every place.

Mona Westergaard

Others, too, have through Aids ministry been prompted to commission songs.

Dr Ian Campbell, when organising the international conference on Aids, commissioned James Anderson to write:

The River of Life

Shores of eternity
   Beckon and call,
Whispering words of love,
   Welcoming all.
There in that land of light,
   City of peace,
Rivers of healing flow.
   Sorrows cease.

There is a river of life
Flowing from God's own Throne,
   Crystal and clear and pure
From God, and God alone.

Jesus, with outstretched hands
   Stands on that shore,
Knowing the stress of life
   He shared before.
Healing is in those hands –
   Touch them and see.
Let him embrace you now.
   Be set free.

Here in the midst of time,
   Lives journey on.
Let all humanity
   Join now as one.
Spirit and source of life,
   Guide us today.
We would belong to you,
   Endlessly

James Anderson

The anguish of suffering and loss, particularly during the phase when many in the United Kingdom were dying, gave rise to some perceptive poetry.

That by William Jesson catches the spirit of the time:

Lyric

Now time is in doubt
And a trap is set that may trip us up.
It's urgent to be alive,
  Not passing the days
Repeating what's known,
Content with the adequate,
  But running with the breeze in our faces
Towards a fresh horizon,
Tasting new scents on the air.

Now time is in doubt
And a trick is laid that may catch us out.
It's urgent to be awake,
  Not sleepwalking
Through tired dreams,
Dulled by the familiar,
  But all the time alert,
The mind's nerve ends tingling,
Savouring the uniqueness of the moment.

Now time is in doubt
And a fault is found that may bring us down.
It's urgent to be flying,
  Not treading through a timetable,
Performing the expected,
Fulfilling the obligation,
  But soaring where the swallow cuts the air,
Headlong in exhilaration,
Riding the breeze in rapture.

I see brothers struggling.
I see friends slip into the flood.
I see those I love swept away.

Let's live,
   Not drifting aimless,
   Not tramping set lines,
   But swept forward by an eager breeze
With prow cutting the surface
In a glistening foam of ecstasy.

Let's live,
   In where the wave is breaking,
   In where the bud is bursting,
   In the unfolding of the moment
Where the stylus tracks the groove
And the music issues forth in its wake.

                  William Jesson

Vivienne Prescott, who helped pioneer the Oasis drop-in centre in Wandsworth, wrote several songs for the annual 'Friends Remembering Friends' services. The following can be sung to the tune of *Repton*:

   I hold a memory within my heart,
   Of sunny days and bright,
   When we would love to laugh and share
   In special moments, without care.
     I promised that we'd never part,
     To hold you in my heart.

   I hold a memory within my heart,
   Of days without the sun.
   The stormy nights and constant rain,
   When I would reach to share your pain.
     I promised that we'd never part,
     To hold you in my heart.

   I hold a memory within my heart,
   A gentle thought of you.
   A precious jewel that grows more rare,
   Each time I turn – and you're not there,
     And yet – I know we'll never part,
     I hold you in my heart.

                  Vivienne Prescott

Cards can be significant for the verses they contain. A card sent to Grant proved of great comfort and has been used in blessing to others on several occasions. Unfortunately, I have been unable to trace the author, to whom I would give credit:

> Let the dreams that are gone sleep fast, my love,
>> Let the tears and fears of yesterdays storm,
> For the darkness you saw is past, my love,
>> So smile and a new day is born.
> The seasons of life will go on, my love,
>> And the sails of your ship may be torn,
> But the secrets beneath your feet, my love,
>> Are the flowers that are yet to be born.
> Let the tears that you shed fall sweet, my love,
>> For the pain goes and rainbows come without warning.
> All the seasons will surely return, my love,
>> And new life will be born in the dawning.
>
> *Anon*

During times when the appearance of many people with Aids was marred by ailments such as acute weight loss and Kaposi's sarcoma, Sonnet CXVI by William Shakespeare has come to mind. Although written about a man and woman in love, somehow it also illustrates the love and devotion I have witnessed in Aids ministry and which by God's grace I have sought to exemplify in my own life:

> Let me not to the marriage of true minds
>> Admit impediments. Love is not love
> Which alters when it alteration finds,
>> Or bends with the remover to remove:
> O, no! it is an ever-fixèd mark,
>> That looks on tempests, and is never shaken;
> It is the star to every wandering bark,
>> Whose worth's unknown, although his height be taken.
> Love's not Time's fool, though rosy lips and cheeks
>> Within his bending sickle's compass come,
> Love alters not with his brief hours and weeks,
>> But bears it out even to the edge of doom.
> If this be error, and upon me proved,
>> I never writ, nor no man ever loved.
>
> *William Shakespeare*

64

16.

Addictions

AMID the hustle and bustle of London's West End, on the south side of Oxford Street, a stone's throw from Oxford Circus, the yellow, red and blue of an Army flag flutters over the passing crowds. Walk beneath it; pass through the entrance over which it flies and you will discover a beautiful auditorium, the Army's Regent Hall. On a Friday lunch time, resisting the temptation of the coffee shop, take a seat in the hall and you will find yourself immersed in a wonderful world of classical sound.

Some years ago, at this same venue, an all night drop-in was held on Friday nights and late into Saturday nights in the youth club premises upstairs. In one corner there was a skiffle group (that shows how long ago!) and in another a bar serving soft drinks and hot dogs, while people relaxed and chatted elsewhere around the modest-sized room. As opportunity permitted I occasionally attended and engaged with others in what might be termed street counselling. There in the room, or sitting on the stairs or pavement kerb outside, I would converse long into the night with all sorts of young men and women, a cross section of society.

World's End

Sometimes I went with Victor Ashworth, an area probation officer. Victor would be in civvies and I in my Salvation Army uniform. People confided more frequently in me because they knew I came from the Army but tended to be a little suspicious of Victor as they were not sure where he came from. Among the customers were a few addicted to illicit drugs and occasionally one or another had to be rushed off to hospital because of an overdose. Some were referred to a drug users' rehabilitation centre run by Betty Care, a Salvation Army officer who operated from a small centre at World's End in Chelsea. I occasionally visited the place to encourage Betty in her pioneering ministry that was supported by a team of doctors in a nearby surgery. Eventually the centre closed, as the NHS increasingly took responsibility for treatment of people addicted to drugs.

Betty, bless her, remained an individualist to the end of her life. She had a flat fronting a walkway above shops in Brick Lane, where some while ago a bomb devastated premises in the roadway below.

When I later visited Betty, she spoke highly of two young gay men who lived nearby and who were always supportive of her. Knowing one of them, who was a medical research scientist, I was glad to hear this comment.

Outpatient

The experiences at Regent Hall and with Betty Care made me more aware that to support and treat people addicted to drugs requires enormous patience and skill. This comes into even sharper focus in Aids ministry in the cases where drug addiction is a factor. Those I have been involved with are desperate to give up their addiction but find it hard to achieve this goal.

There can be particular problems when it comes to outpatient treatment. The ability and willingness to take prescribed drugs as and when needed may be a vexed issue, conflicting with the overwhelming desire for other, illicit drugs.

Inpatient

Inpatient treatment, on the other hand, may lead to problems for other patients due to the disruptive nature of some drug users. Occasionally there can be pressure to give loans of money, for the purchase of drugs – loans that are seldom returned. Anxious to get money for illegal drugs, patients may rob from other patients in the ward. So there is need to safeguard personal possessions and to refuse requests for loans. All this can be disconcerting for other patients, who want to concentrate on improving health, and a vexed issue for nurses.

For relations and friends, it can be heartbreaking to see a loved one's life blighted by the abuse of drugs, particularly if they have contracted HIV as a result of drug use. But above all, drug users are people – people, who by choice or not have found themselves ensnared in the drugs habit, the dupes of those who gain financially from their addiction.

And people matter.

Alcohol

Alcohol, of course, is the drug that ensnares most people, costing the United Kingdom far more than illegal drugs do. Time and again I have taken friends to a variety of centres in London and as far away as *Clouds* in Wiltshire to be 'dried out' and rehabilitated. Thankfully, many have reduced their consumption and some have given up altogether, their lives transformed.

To be a friend and carer for people with Aids, who are also alcoholics, can be a real test. I know what it's like to have bottles hidden from me but then to reach a stage when trust is such that bottles are no longer hidden. Reluctantly, I have at times bought alcohol, knowing that if I didn't then larger bottles would be purchased!

Marcus

One day, I paused at the traffic lights in Marchmont Street, waiting for them to change. A young man beside me was in a distressed state and, with tears in his eyes, asked to speak with me. I accepted his invitation to go to a nearby café for a coffee and chat. Recently bereaved of a friend who had Aids, Marcus had resorted to alcohol. But this brought no consolation. Alcoholism was obviously an additional problem with which he was contending.

We conversed at length but I realised more prolonged support would be necessary. Later in the day, I called at his flat and rang the intercom. He was in a paranoid state, his imagination running riot, and I was unable to gain admission. I waited for an opportunity when he was less fraught. Further visits and conversations resulted in an introduction to another friend. As a result, I was able to take both men to the funeral of another friend who had died. A link-up with Chalk Farm Oasis drop-in, at that time held in the Chalk Farm Salvation Army hall, provided another source of fellowship and support, plus good meals. Continued contact with Marcus also resulted in him making occasional visits to my office, where he became known to some of the staff.

Needing to make occasional visits to a person in Aldershot, I invited Marcus to accompany me. He suffered with asthma, so it did him good to get away from London and gave him opportunities to visit his mother in Basingstoke. She is now an avid reader of the Army's weekly periodicals *The War Cry, Salvationist* and *Kids Alive!* that I pass on via Marcus.

In addition to the occasional journeys south of London, Marcus and a friend have also accompanied me to my hometown of Cheltenham for a weekend, returning to the city the better for the break away.

And alcohol? Marcus no longer needs it, and can manage fine well without it.

Smoking

A further addiction for many is, of course, smoking – and what a lot of people wish they could give up that habit! Smoking makes someone with Aids more susceptible to bronchial problems. Frequently doctors urge patients to give up or reduce smoking. However, if a person is terminally ill it is too late and smoking may be one of their few last pleasures!

I guess there are all sorts of addictions. Well, enough, I must have a cup of tea!

17.

Rape

D EALING with the aftermath of the rape or attempted rape of men and women is an issue I've been faced with on a number of occasions in Aids ministry. The invasion of the privacy and security of one's home by a burglar can be a traumatic experience. Even if nothing of real worth is stolen, the very sense that a stranger has touched and contaminated your possessions can be distasteful in the extreme.

Such reactions and emotions are all the more real for people who have been raped or have experienced attempted rape. They have been personally violated.

Few cases actually come to court, let alone result in a conviction. As it is, conviction rates are at present very low, arousing much government and police concern. Men, in particular, have been reluctant to go to the police, for fear of a hostile reception. Thankfully, in recent years much has changed in regard to police responses and the support of men and women who have experienced such traumas.

Imagine the trauma of a woman raped. But what if as a consequence she has become infected with HIV and therefore risks developing Aids? Horrific! And if in addition she is expecting a child? The mind boggles at the thought of all the issues with which she contends, needing not only professional support but also the support of friends and relations.

The risk of infection by HIV is one of the reasons why Wandsworth Oasis Trading Company Limited, which supports people who have been affected by HIV, agreed to sponsor the production costs of *Hope Beyond Hurt – Supporting People who have been Raped*. I will not write at length on this subject. Suffice to say I can speak from practical experience of supporting people.

On one occasion it was no easy thing to take the stand in a Crown Court and testify in support of a Crown case. I was aware that there are times when testimonies can be distorted and undermined by the defence, causing hurt to the testifier. I felt as if I was putting my job on the line. There I stood, quietly confident in the truth, wearing my Salvation Army uniform. I felt something like the young man who was servant to Elisha in the Old Testament and feared the onslaught of the enemy, causing the prophet to pray:

'Lord, I pray thee, open his eyes, that he may see.'
And the Lord opened the eyes of the young man; and he saw: and, behold, the mountain was full of horses and chariots of fire round about Elisha.

(2 Kings 6:17, *KJV*).

The experience in court was all the more traumatic for the man against whom the incident of rape had taken place. And it entailed giving additional support over many months. Thankfully, he also was strong in personal faith.

Hope Beyond Hurt

Hope Beyond Hurt
Supporting a person who has been raped
Author Trevor A. Smith

Hope Beyond Hurt may be a useful tool for relations and friends who seek to be supportive of people who have been raped, as well as people who have experienced rape.

This booklet, published in 2002, is available from:

The Salvation Army
Social Services,
Territorial Headquarters
101 Newington Causeway
London SE1 6BN.

(Price £1 to cover post/administration)

18.

Uniform

THERE'S an indefinable 'something' about a bedside manner. Diana, Princess of Wales had it. For the princess, royal status was not a barrier. Her Majesty The Queen also has this gift, making people feel that they matter, even though the contact may be brief. Hospital chaplains and others co-operating in the healing art value this gift. Those engaged in teaching nurses, as well as others in caring professions, would doubtless have textbook descriptions of what it is. As for me, I learned a little of the art as a medic in the Royal Air Force, and needed it desperately when undertaking ministry to those with Aids.

It should not be something contrived but the natural outcome of a caring personality. Eye level contact is important but, in a sense, it is the heart-to-heart level contact that matters most.

I shall ever be grateful for the chance meeting with Andrew, together with his partner, sister and friends, when I was visiting another patient in Mildmay Mission Hospital. As with so many other people, I regret I did not know him in better times, when his life had not been blighted by Aids.

Originating from a Greek family, his dark features enhanced his good looks. As Samuel, the prophet, remarked to Jesse when considering his sons with a view to anointing one of them as the future king of Israel,

Man looketh on the outward appearance, but the Lord looketh on the heart
(1 Samuel 16:7, *KJV*).

In the case of Andrew, I was convinced that the inner man conformed to the outer man and certainly his warm and pleasant personality evinced this fact. Even though my association with Andrew lasted a comparatively short time, his death saddened me greatly and I felt all the more for his loved ones. Their sorrow was deep and sincere.

71

I readily attended his funeral service at the Greek Orthodox Church, which for me was a moving and learning experience, as I am sure it was for his work colleagues, who also attended. As I later remarked to his partner,

> That he concluded his days surrounded by so much love and care is something for which to be very grateful . . . To sit quietly with him for just over half an hour, just holding his hand, while you and others were busy elsewhere, is an experience I'll reflect on with thankfulness.

Later still, Andrew's partner wrote:

> The talks we had were very comforting at a time when I felt desperate. I am lucky to have met you. Thank you so much. More especially my thanks are for the way you helped Andy. I remember the happiness on his face when he would see you and the affection in the way he kissed you and reached out to hold your hand when you talked. I was so glad that you were around not just to cheer him up but to comfort him and talk with him, as death came closer, in a way he couldn't talk to anyone else, including me. You seemed to reach Andy in a way I had never seen anyone do before.

I was moved and thankful that the Lord could use me in this way. Uniform was certainly no barrier to a depth of shared understanding. It is testimony to the affection in which Andrew was held that when his sister Maria, now living in Athens, gave birth to a boy, she named him Andrew.

From the earliest years of ministry to people affected by Aids, I was determined to wear uniform most of the time, so that the Army was seen to be involved with them. In one sense it was not me – it was the Army, showing its commitment to care at a time of harsh voices and hostility from many sides. In addition, by wearing uniform I was paving the way for others to be involved.

And is uniform a barrier to ministry? Seldom, if ever. If there is any barrier, it could be the person wearing the uniform, not the uniform itself.

I must confess a preference to nurses wearing uniform, rather than civvies. In establishments where civvies have been in vogue, even as a regular visitor I've had difficulty in differentiating between patients and nurses, let alone between patients and visitors. In my opinion, there's something about nurses wearing uniform that inspires in patients a greater degree of confidence, plus the fact that I like to identify people by name and an easy-to-read name badge helps.

Perhaps I'm getting too old in the tooth!

19.

World Aids Day Services

A S THE toll on human life increased, so did candlelight vigils, inter-faith and ecumenical services. World Aids Day services in London and elsewhere in the country, highlighted the involvement of Christian faith communities, to be joined later by representatives of both Jewish and Muslim faith communities. In 1989, Peter Harris, Krystyna Fuchs and colleagues within Catholic Aids Link, together with the Reverend Pat Wright and other representatives of various churches, organised a World Aids Day service in St George's Cathedral, Southwark to take place on Friday 1 December. I took part as one of two ministers engaged in the laying on of hands for those wishing to come forward for prayer and blessing – a gesture which reminded me of Salvation Army practice, where people come to the mercy seat for a similar type of ministry. In an adjacent hall, a modest exhibition was staged by Aids organisations, including Wandsworth Oasis. The presence of the then Minister for Health, Mrs Virginia Bottomley MP, showed how government concern was growing about the issue of Aids.

Michael came with me to this event. The night was cold – almost as cold, so it seemed, inside the cathedral as out – which gave me cause for concern for Michael's health, as I had taken him in my car. However, the spirit of the occasion was good and, thankfully, Michael appeared none the worse for the experience.

In March 1990, the Reverend Malcolm A. Johnson invited me to a meeting at St Botolph-without-Aldgate, where he was Rector, to discuss the next World Aids Day service, to be held in Westminster Abbey on Friday 30 November. The group comprised people involved in ministry to people affected by Aids and represented a number of denominations. The eventual 'Service of Hope' proved effective, enhanced by the fellowship and refreshments available afterwards in Westminster Central Hall.

The international theme for the year was *Women and Aids*. Something of a prophetic move, as at that time Aids was generally thought of as predominantly a male affliction. Recent figures show, however, that the worldwide prevalence of Aids is now split 50/50 and the number of women affected is growing more rapidly than the number of men.

To mark World Aids Day, religious and non-religious events have been held year by year at local level throughout the country. I was personally involved in 1990 when the Hillingdon Borough Council in conjunction with local churches initiated a *Christian Response to Aids* event, held in Uxbridge SA hall. Richard Durrant, the local Army leader asked me to speak briefly and engage in the afternoon gathering of worship, discussion, information and intercession.

In 1991 a World Aids Day service took place in Southwark Cathedral, where St Andrew's Chapel is designated as 'a place of prayer for all who live and die under the shadow of HIV and Aids'. A drama, *Alone*, by Vivienne from Wandsworth, was performed by representatives of Wandsworth Oasis during the service. It resulted in a front-page photograph in *The Independent*, showing Colin acting centre stage.

During that period of the year, I attended the Living for Tomorrow conference, convened by the National Aids Trust and the Health Education Authority, in the presence of Diana, Princess of Wales. The Secretary of State for Education, Kenneth Clarke MP, took part in the final session, chaired by Jonathan Dimbleby.

The 1992 World Aids Day ecumenical service, with its theme 'A Community Commitment', was held in The Salvation Army's Regent Hall, Oxford Street. In successive years the event reverted to Southwark Cathedral, where it seemed to have found its natural 'home', organised for many years by the London Ecumenical Aids Trust.

In 1999 the National Aids Trust organised an event in the Covent Garden Market West Piazza, alongside the rear of St Paul's (The Actors') Church, to mark World Aids Day. Richard and Pauline Cook, leaders of our work in Harlesden, manned the Army's emergency vehicle parked within the grounds of the church. Refreshments were readily available to anyone associated with the event, which attracted a large crowd.

In 2002 the Southwark Cathedral service was matched by another service at the same time in St Paul's Cathedral. Many from both congregations joined afterwards with lighted candles on the Millennium Bridge. On a cold winter's evening, and having Joe and Keith with me, I decided for health reasons not to engage in such a chilling witness!

Year by year, World Aids Day services are welcomed as a means of highlighting the need for a spiritual ministry to people affected by Aids.

Colin acting centre stage, Southwark Cathedral (see opposite)

Left:
'Names Project' Quilts
8 October 1988
Washington DC

Below:
'Names Project' Quilts
Chalk Farm, London
(see page 81)

Below: General Eva Burrows with me, Shane, Philip and Michael (see page 102)

20.

Courageous People

THE courage of many people is amazing. True, some people faced with the daunting prospect of major illness give way under the weight of its onslaught – sometimes otherwise strong people, not used to ill health. The majority, however, draw upon inner resources, often surprising themselves.

I've known Joe ever since he was manager of the Leigh Street Café, near the Army's former Judd Street headquarters, where I worked for a time. I enjoyed my visits to Joe's as the décor, cleanliness and food were all of a high standard. The conversation, too, was good.

I used to meet and chat with Joe and family members. When Joe's father died, I was invited to the funeral and read prayers in the Roman Catholic Church of St Joseph's, Wembley, then went to Ruislip Crematorium. There, the service concluded with a recording of Frank Sinatra singing 'I Did It My Way'. Though the hymns in the services might have been sung with a degree of hesitancy, this popular song was picked up and sung with gusto. It was great. It was a means of uniting the congregation in the tonic of a united spirit.

Time came when Joe's circumstances changed and Aids necessitated relinquishing full time work. Nevertheless he maintained an active life – Chloe, his Labrador dog, made sure of that! His home reflects the high standards he maintained in the café and I still enjoy his hospitality. Joe is not going to let ill health defeat him!

As if not coping with enough, Joe developed non-Hodgkin's lymphoma – cancer. Admitted to the Royal Free Hospital, where I continued to visit him, he underwent surgery, radiotherapy and chemotherapy. Those were tough times, not only because of the illness but also because of the side effects, with loss of hair and gaunt features.

Joe and Chloe

Thankfully, Joe is now in complete remission in regard to cancer and is looking so well that no one meeting him for the first time would realise that day by day he is still living with Aids.

There is a uniquely close bond between Joe and Mollie, his second dog. When Mollie recently had a major operation, Joe cared for her as if she was a child. The dog showed similar resilience to her master and is now fully recovered. Walkies are in vogue again!

Joe gave a moving testimony at a recent World Aids Day service in Wandsworth SA hall, organised by the Wandsworth Oasis Trading Company Limited. He continues to donate items for the Oasis charity shops, and encourages others to do likewise.

Irene was an industrious member of the Aids organisation Body Positive, serving on management committees and representing the women's group. In those early pioneering years, Body Positive had a predominantly male leadership, so Irene's role was crucial in representing women's interests. In addition, she was on the rota for those manning the telephone helpline, always ready to respond if a colleague wanted to refer a woman caller to her.

On her way back home to her flat near the River Thames late one evening, Irene was mugged by several men, who kicked, punched and robbed her. It left her in a bad state slumped to the ground, not far from her home.

The mugging was an all the more grievous happening in view of the fact that Irene was not in good health. Thankfully, she was admitted to Mildmay Mission Hospital, where she received much tender loving care. When I visited Irene in hospital, she exhibited the same courageous spirit she had shown through the years.

Feeling unsafe to continue living in her flat, Irene decided to return to her family home in Doncaster, where she eventually died, in 1992, in Doncaster Royal Infirmary. Courageous to the end, her death was a sad loss not only to Body Positive but also to many individuals whom she had helped along the way.

Unable to attend the funeral service in Doncaster, I sent a message, part of which read:

> Irene was a person of strong convictions and determined attitude, which prompted her zealous concern for the wellbeing of other people. She strove hard to improve the lot of people disadvantaged by health and other circumstance, being particularly mindful of women who found it difficult to voice their concerns.
>
> Courage was the hallmark of Irene, not only as she strove in the interests of other people but also as she wrestled with her own declining health. I recall visiting her in hospital and at home following the severe mugging she received one night, after she had been busy in the interests of others and was wending her way home through Chelsea. That experience, courageously borne, left Irene shaken in more ways than one and prompted her to talk further about the possibility of moving to Doncaster.

It took courage, too, for Irene on her own initiative to ask me to talk with her about funeral arrangements if she remained in London. She had obviously given it prior thought, suggesting her fondness for the hymns 'The Old Rugged Cross' and 'The Lord's My Shepherd' and the fact that the hymn 'Morning Has Broken' sounded a buoyant, optimistic theme. Psalm 121 'I will lift up my eyes to the hills' was also mentioned as expressing such faith as she had. Before I departed from her home, she asked me to pray and we both sensed the safe refuge that her home had become and also her need of a quiet heart and mind.

I later conducted a memorial service in the beautiful chapel in Mildmay Mission Hospital, attended by some of Irene's friends in London. A substantial sum of money was raised on that occasion and this was sent to Ruth Sims, Chief Executive of Mildmay who, in a letter of thanks, stated, 'I knew Irene in those early days of Mildmay's re-opening, both when she was quite well and when she became really ill. We often used to talk on the phone. She was a great help to me in understanding the pain, loneliness and rejection experienced by people with Aids.'

Especially in the early years of the Aids pandemic, people not only had to be courageous in coping with a life-threatening illness but very often had to cope with prejudice, fear and hostility. The prejudice, fear and hostility often spilled over to those supporting people with HIV/Aids.

In November 1987, a team from Aksept Kontaktsenter, Oslo, Norway, led by the manager, Helge Fiskness, came to London to learn more about how to respond to the emerging pandemic of Aids.

They visited a number of centres and also came to have lunch with me at the Salvation Army headquarters in Queen Victoria Street.

It was a pleasure to meet such a genial group, anxious to be supportive of people with Aids, learning all they could from the visit to London in order to better equip them for the task ahead.

Henki

As Helge remarked in a letter:

Just having met you all, who are involved with the same challenge as we are facing, gave us a lot of inspiration which I suppose will be a resource in itself.

One member of the team was Henki, a young man living with Aids with whom I established an immediate rapport. I was very conscious of his courage in being up front about his illness so that he could be supportive of other people. In those early years it took courage to declare publicly that you had Aids and were prepared to respond to media interviews; that you wanted to focus public attention on the issue and be supportive of people who could not risk going public.

The contact with Henki was brief, as the team departed for other centres after the meal, but I was able to encourage him by letter, and practically with the small gift of a pillbox timer.

Sadly, all too soon, in June 1989 I received a letter from his sister, Ulla, telling me Henki had died. Ulla later sent me a photograph together with a book that had been written about him – although I would need to learn Norwegian in order to read it! I will always associate the word courage with that young man, Henki.

21.

Welcome Guests – animals

PETS, particularly dogs and cats, may be of comfort to people who are ill or aged. My parents' pet dog, Fudge, was always a welcome guest in the home of my elderly aunt, who revelled in the opportunity to give it dainty morsels to eat. In contrast the family's pet cat was not so welcome! We had to admit it sat on the edge of the pond and played 'hooky' with the fish, with the result of diminishing their number!

James, the first person I was involved with in Aids ministry, had two beautiful, sleek black cats. I would love to have adopted them, but it would not have been practical. As health declined and he went in and out of hospital, my friend knew the time had come to part company and ensure the cats went to a pleasant country home.

It was like a bereavement for him.

Martin and Gilbert had two cats. Bluie was an attractive demure little lady and shyly hid behind the settee whenever I visited. The other, Tinker, was adventurous and likely to be found stranded on a nearby roof! When Martin died, his partner felt obliged to part with these two delightful pets, so a friend adopted them into his family of cats. Both cats, now less timorous, hurry to join the others in greeting me on arrival at his home. They have now become 'family'.

What should happen to Stan's boisterous dog when the time came for him to be found a home? The dog had always made me welcome even if, when jumping up, his front paws seemed intent on injuring my most tender area! Thankfully, a boisterous family was found to match his energies. Yet the parting reinforced Stan's awareness of declining health and diminshing prospect of returning home.

It was a further psychological blow with which to cope.

Occasionally, with appropriate safeguards, nursing staff allow pet dogs to be brought to visit their masters. Much depends upon the type and control of the pet and the setting in which it takes place. But why needlessly suffer a sense of bereavement before possible death, due to inability to see a much loved pet? It can mean so much to both patient and dog. What a tonic for a patient!

Chris had a pure white West Highland Terrier. It was always a joy to meet that bright little dog when visiting Chris or meeting him in the foyer of London Lighthouse, where the dog captivated the hearts of everyone. Tragic the day when Chris was bereaved of the dog.

We had all lost a friend.

Children's allowances help parents cope with the expenditure required for food, clothing, etc, for their growing offspring. For a single person coping with health problems and dependent on State benefits, it is no small consideration to face the expenditure on pet food. It is too glib to suggest they part with pets that have become 'family' and which bring comfort during hours of loneliness and sometimes depression. I wish some means could be found of making financial assistance available in cases of genuine need without people feeling that they are begging, which could add further stress to their already stressful lives.

On another scale of things, in 1994 I conducted a funeral service at London Lighthouse followed by the commital in West London Crematorium, Kensal Green. Neil Cocking and his colleagues at Chelsea Funeral Directors, Fulham Road, arranged for a Victorian hearse drawn by magnificent black horses. It was a beautiful sunny day and, despite it being a funeral, the procession with the horse-drawn hearse made an impressive sight, attracting many people along the road as we wended our way to the crematorium. Not an easy achievement amidst the London traffic, but all went well.

Sometimes there are unfinished stories regarding pets. Little notices on trees and lampposts pleading for news of a missing cat or dog leave one wondering if there is a satisfactory outcome. David had a very boisterous mongrel, something like a cross between a Labrador and Alsatian. It always made me very welcome, even if I did appear to be wearing a fur coat afterwards! One day, as was his custom, David took this young dog for a walk on a nearby common. Chasing around all over the place, the dog did not heed David's call for it to return to his side and, search and call as he might, he never found the animal. It had disappeared into the sunset. He was left wondering if it had found a better home, perhaps attracted by a mate.

Thereafter David made the most of a frog that had made its home in a crevice beside the pond in his garden!

22.

Artistic Design

URING the early years of the Aids pandemic, friends and families
sought to give tangible expression to the remembrance of loved
ones by making quilts. No, not the type for putting on beds! These
measure six feet by three feet and comprise a sheet of material, into
which pieces of material and other items are sewn, so that the quilt
reflects the life of and becomes a tribute to the deceased.

Some quilts have become skilled works of art, reflecting the esteem
in which people were held. They have often been exhibited in churches
and cathedrals during World Aids Day services; at special services in
Westminster Abbey, and there was also a huge exhibition of quilts in
Hyde Park. Wandsworth Oasis and Chalk Farm Oasis were among
centres where quilts were made and were exhibited on such occasions as
annual 'Friends Remembering Friends' services.

Art, particularly painting, is used as a means of therapy for people
with Aids, just as with people who have other illnesses. Mildmay Mission
Hospital, for example, found art to be therapeutic for many patients.

In centuries past and in a more limited way today, stained glass
windows in churches and cathedrals have been a means of
communicating the history and teachings of the Bible. Despite massive
technological changes, paintings and other forms of artwork remain
excellent means of communicating with people.

Crusaid, a highly respected organisation that raises funds to support
people affected by Aids, has used André Durand's painting *Votive Offering*
and Brian Masters's copyright write-up as a means of raising funds. The
painting was taken on a tour of England, being exhibited in churches and
cathedrals. For centuries, votive offerings, including those within the
Christian Church, have been a means of fulfilling vows and consecrating
to God the creative work of human hands. Used with permission and
slightly adapted, an extract from Brian Masters' write-up reads:

At the beginning of 1986, André Durand was inspired by the beauty and personality of an effervescent and joyful young legal secretary, called Sonya Sherman, and determined he would paint her portrait. He did not then know that, at 35, 'Sunnye' had only months to live. She was dying of what threatened to be the modern plague of Aids. When he discovered this, he vowed to dedicate his painting as an offering, a prayer for salvation from the disease. Sunnye, too, vowed to leave a legacy of good. 'I ask God,' she said, 'to extend my life long enough to reach certain goals.'

Sonnye Sherman is now dead but her vow has been translated into Durand's painting. Adapting the classical iconography of a Renaissance altarpiece, he depicts an imaginary meeting. Miss Sherman is in hospital receiving Diana, Princess of Wales, attended by St George, the patron saint of England; and St Sebastian and St Catherine of Genoa, both traditionally called upon in time of plague. St Catherine devoted twenty years to nursing the sick in the Pammatone hospital, eventually moving in to live with them as matron. Her devotion to the plague-stricken nearly cost her life. She died in 1510 and was canonised in 1737.

The presence of Diana, Princess of Wales, introduces another manifestation of faith. She inherited the scarcely acknowledged tradition of the healing power of royalty, which dates from Edward the Confessor. Charles II 'touched' over 90,000 people during his reign – usually sufferers from tuberculosis – about 20 each day. It was a solemn ceremony to the accompaniment of the royal chaplain's richly intoned words, 'He laid his hands upon them and healed them.' Dr Johnson was taken as a child to be 'touched' by Queen Anne. Diana, Princess of Wales, demonstrated her care for those with Aids by visiting patients in hospital, so it is entirely appropriate that Durand's vision should show her 'touching' the subject by resting a gentle hand on Sunnye Sherman's arm. The pilgrimage of *Votive Offering* through the cathedral cities of England offered an opportunity for collaboration between artist and worshippers in beseeching God to 'turn away' the scourge of Aids. That the cathedrals should host such a prayer is not surprising, for the artist aspires to the proper aim of achieving a miracle through a painting.

I recall going with my dear friend Guy to the exhibition *The Image of Christ* at the National Gallery, London. The event attracted thousands of people and we joined them, intrigued by the skills of the artists and the many forms in which Jesus Christ is portrayed.

At the end of the exhibition, my friend whose life expectancy was now limited as a result of Aids stood for a long while before Salvador Dali's painting *Christ of St John of the Cross*. It was a moving moment for both of us and we needed no words to communicate our thoughts. It was a reminder that it is not the nails but love that holds Christ to the Cross, a love poured out for all people, including my friend.

Above: Votive Offering by André Durand
(see opposite)

Left: Princess Diana, ready with knife in hand

Right: Helping Colin cut the cake
(see pages 89,90)

Above: Chatting to Michael Kelly at Mildmay, 20 November 1991 (see page 39)

Below: With Philip, 13 September 1988, opening of the Kobler Centre (see page 101)

23.

Saying it with Flowers

DAVID was a highly skilled, good-looking young man of 32 years who had experienced much hurt and sadness in his short life. I wish I had known him in better times. He was a determined fellow who, though terribly frail, would ask me to drive him to Hammersmith. He'd get out of the car and struggle through the underpass to the Post Office to draw his State benefits. On one occasion, despite purple blemishes of Kaposi's sarcoma being so obvious on his face and scalp, I took him to the hairdressers in Earls Court, heedful of the looks of customers. Thank God for an understanding hairdresser, who treated David like any other client, with no hint of hesitation.

It reached the stage when David became angry and would not allow his few friends to visit him in the side room of the Westminster Hospital ward. At one point he wouldn't even let Mrs Marguerite van Doren, his charming and competent 'Buddy', visit him. His anger was understandable as he had been a young professional, anticipating a long, fulfilled life, but now his body was frail and he had become totally blind. Writing at a later date, Marguerite says:

After David decided not to see me, I still kept going to the hospital, only to be refused a visit each time. The constant rejection was hard to bear, as we had been so close. However, I did by chance meet you on one of those unsuccessful visits, and you managed to persuade me that it was David's suffering and anguish which were causing him to lash out, and that it was nothing to do with me personally. It was hard to believe that it was nothing I had done. I was convinced it was my fault and spent many sleepless nights wondering what I had done to make David – as I perceived it then – turn against me. In the end, through you, I came to terms with this 'rejection' by David. Your words gave me a different perspective, and I began to realise how important it was for him to live the remaining days as he wanted and

83

not how I wanted. I realised that perhaps he was coming closer to God, that he needed to focus on that as the time drew nearer for him to go. He saw you as someone who truly understood him and who could guide him through his journey towards God. Through you he had found his spirituality and that had become very important to him.

Having come to terms with his refusal to see me, I found to my astonishment when I next visited the hospital that he wanted to see me!

You were the one to break the good news to me and I went to his bedside. David was very ill by this time and not very coherent but I was able to assist the nurse in turning him over. David recognised me with a flicker of a smile and we touched hands. It remains to this day so very important that I was able to say goodbye to David and thank him for all the joy he had given me as his Buddy.

Thankfully, David allowed me to continue visiting him and on one occasion Sister Una Conran FCJ, a hospital volunteer, came into the room. Of mature years and very much down to earth, this former lecturer for the Terrence Higgins Trust is a member of the Roman Catholic order of the Faithful Companions of Jesus. On a previous occasion, David had permitted her to say the Lord's Prayer with him and on this occasion readily agreed for us to do so again. Forming a prayer circle by holding each other's hands, we said the prayer together.

It was a moving moment.

Permission to die

On visiting David another day, it was obvious his life was ebbing to its close. Sensitive to the moment, I said to him, 'David, if in your mind's eye you perceive a light to which you should respond, or a door through which you should go, go for it, my love, and God bless you.' And with that he peacefully died. There are times when it seems right to give a person permission to die, so they do not feel obliged to hold back, and they take that final journey into the next life, reassured that all is well for their onward journey.

There were few people at his funeral but afterwards Marguerite wrote:

The whole programme was David from beginning to end. I'm sure I am speaking for everyone when I say this and I'm sure each and every one of us was brought very close to David during that half hour. The lovely gesture of offering flowers to him was one that David himself would have adored and would have found great pleasure in. But the thought that went into that – and I am referring to the colour of the flowers you chose – made it such a very personal moment for me especially. The choice of everything was just right. Each reading and each word of your own oration so lovingly embraced each of us who had been close to David. Thank you so much, Trevor. I will keep my memory of that morning always, as well as the programme you so painstakingly laid out for us to follow.

John, David's social worker, remarked in a letter, 'David's wish was that he would be remembered.' I, for one, remember him with deep respect and affection.

Voluntary tributes

By means of planned tributes during funeral services, people *are* remembered with respect and affection. In addition, I have usually allowed time for voluntary tributes and this has never failed. Members of the congregation have stood and briefly expressed a pleasing memory of the one whose life is celebrated. Sometimes this includes a respectful joke about them. On one occasion a young man came forward to briefly sing his tribute. On another occasion a mother and father stepped forward, hand in hand, to give a glowing word of tribute to their beloved son. All this and more has been the stuff of sincere and moving tributes

Conducting funerals for people who have died as a result of Aids has given rise to several ways of involving the congregation and in this flowers have had a role.

Chicken wire had a place in funeral planning!

In the early years of the Aids pandemic, sufficient chicken wire would be purchased to drape over a coffin. Then it would be interwoven with greenery, so that the wire could not be seen. On arrival for the service, everyone was given a single rose or carnation. During the service they were invited to come forward, to the accompaniment of music, to place their floral tributes within the greenery. The final effect was a beautiful floral carpet over the coffin. It was a way of involving everyone and, unable to voice a tribute, they could 'Say it with flowers' in this unique way.

The big drawback was that nothing could be done with the floral tribute after the service except lay it on the ground, to be admired by everyone. A more acceptable means of involving everyone needed to be devised, so I consulted Valerie of Valerie's Flowers in the Portobello Road,

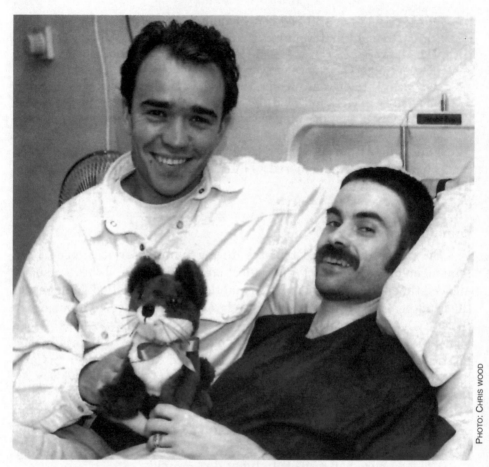

Colin with Todd Carty at Mildmay

PHOTO: CHRIS WOOD

who suggested that a florist's pedestal column should be purchased, or to use a small table on which to place a bowl containing some oasis. Sprigs of greenery would be planted in the oasis, resulting in an attractive arrangement. At the appropriate moment in the service, the congregation was invited to place their flowers in this arrangement – or in two arrangements if a large congregation was anticipated. It was more attractive and more practical, as afterwards it could be presented to the hospital in which the deceased had been a patient.

The important thing was that it involved the congregation as a whole.

Valerie went the extra mile. It was not unknown for her to visit patients, at their request, in the residential unit of London Lighthouse, in Lancaster Road, to ascertain their wishes regarding flowers for their own funeral. The Lighthouse is a modern drop-in and support centre. At that time the building, which had been officially opened by HRH Princess Margaret, also had a residential facility offering respite and terminal care.

When Todd Carty, who played the role of Mark in EastEnders, wanted to learn more about Aids, so that he could act his part more effectively, he visited Mildmay Mission Hospital. There he met Colin, who later became a patient in London Lighthouse.

Planned funeral

Mindful of his limited life expectancy, Colin asked for a Bible to read and learn more. In addition, he meticulously planned his funeral order of service, including a message I was to read to his mother and father. An extract reads:

> Try not to be sad. I've only left this world to go on to a higher spiritual level. I will be around you from time to time to watch over you. I know one day we shall all be together again.

Enjoying a respite period back in his home, he was overjoyed to renew love and friendship with Willem from The Netherlands. I was glad to visit them just before they departed for that country to spend Christmas together. Unexpectedly, Colin rapidly declined in health. Having advised him to contact The Salvation Army if any problems arose, my colleague at the Netherlands Headquarters, Ron Thomlinson, visited Willem and Colin. At their request he prayed with them and, alas, ultimately conducted Colin's funeral in The Netherlands, continuing to minister to Willem afterwards.

Family and friends gathered in the Ian McKellen Hall at London Lighthouse for a Service of Thanksgiving and Reflection. Colin had wanted a huge floral rainbow and, in anticipation of his funeral, had placed an order with Valerie. Making a strong wire skeleton of a rainbow, 65 inches across, fulfilled the order. Moss was fixed to it and this was covered with countless blooms. It looked marvellous, pleasing to the eye, and impressed everyone – and doubtless pleased Colin, as he looked over the ramparts of Heaven! The only problem was what to do with it after I'd conducted the service. Back it went to the shop, where it hung on the wall, to be admired by customers until the accumulation of cobwebs suggested the need to dispose of the rainbow. Rainbows do have an ending, even if there isn't a pot of gold there!

Colin's rainbow reminded me of H. W. Longfellow's poem *The Song of Hiawatha* and the extract about the rainbow, recalling how Nokomis the old nurse taught the child many things about nature and the world around him:

> Saw the rainbow in the heaven,
> In the eastern sky, the rainbow,
> Whispered, 'What is that, Nokomis?'
> And the good Nokomis answered:
> 'Tis the heaven of flowers you see there;
> All the wild-flowers of the forest,
> All the lilies of the prairie,
> When on earth they fade and perish,
> Blossom in that heaven above us.'

Princess visiting

The colour photographs opposite page 82 show Diana, Princess of Wales visiting Colin in London Lighthouse, so when his Service of Thanksgiving and Reflection was being prepared it seemed appropriate to send her an advance copy.

A letter came in response from her Private Secretary, Patrick Jephson:

20 January 1992

Dear Major Smith,

The Princess of Wales has asked me to thank you for
your very kind letter of 16th January about Colin.
Her Royal Highness's sadness at his death was
tempered by the knowledge – gained during her brief
visit to him at London Lighthouse – that he
approached it in peace and hope.
Thank you again for taking the trouble to write.
Yours sincerely,

(Signed)
Patrick Jephson

To the surprise and pleasure of everyone present, a little before the service commenced a modest but beautiful floral arrangement was delivered with a card from the Princess.

Such a gesture did not hit the headlines in the press but it meant so much to everyone present. So there we had a small table draped with a rainbow flag, on which was placed Colin's framed photograph and the princess's floral tribute. Colin's father has given permission for me to quote from his letter which movingly describes the visit of Diana, Princess of Wales, to his son:

17 February 2003

Dear Trevor,

. . . one day, while I was with Colin at the Lighthouse, he asked me to draw up his will, whilst his mother, stepmother and buddy were away for tea. This in itself was difficult for me, being his father. Having finished it, I asked him whether there was anything special he would like me to do for him. Colin being Colin said, 'Yes, Dad. I would like to meet Princess Diana.'
Wow! How does one get about this!
When I got home, I wrote several letters to her equerry and tore them all up and finally wrote to her direct, because I understood that she opened her own mail. The princess phoned me at home the following morning. My wife took the call and when she asked who was calling the princess merely said, 'Diana!'
I had just left for my office, so she phoned me again, at my office, and arranged to call on Colin at the Lighthouse – but not to tell them she was going to call. The date and time was arranged and she duly arrived and was shown to a special room and we were invited and went downstairs, from the residential unit, to this room to meet her.
The Princess opened the door and the girls – Valerie, Patsy and Biddy started to curtsy, not knowing whether to put the right leg behind the left or vice versa. She responded by saying, 'Oh please, forget that, do come in.'

The Princess put everyone at ease. There was a percussion group next door making quite a lot of noise, to which she said, 'Sounds like Phil Collins is warming up!' She said she had never received such a moving letter from a father with regard to his son and this put everyone at ease. As a mere man, watching her and the women talking was like watching a girls' reunion. When Patsy remarked, 'I noticed in the newspaper that you had come second in the mothers' race at Harry's school,' she said, 'Yes, but the winner cheated!'

We had brought a home-made birthday cake for Colin, in the shape of a teddy bear. We offered the Princess a piece, which she accepted and then we realised we had no plate. She said, 'No matter, cut me off a piece and put it in the serviette. I'll eat it before I get back to Kensington Palace anyway.'

She spent over half an hour with Colin, talking with him. She had brought him a wooden bowl of scented candles (appropriate later, bearing in mind 'Candle in the Wind') and said that she and Harry had chosen it for him that morning. She was loving, caring and attentive to Colin. When she was departing, Colin gave her a bunch of red roses.

I personally saw her out of the room. She stopped and said to me personally, 'How are you coping?' to which I replied, 'Well, you're a Mum and I'm a Dad (forgetting all protocol). I have good days and bad days but I have to remain strong for him.'

She replied, 'I want you to write to me and keep me informed how he is.' I thanked her for her kindness in coming. She stopped at every door she went through, then turned round and waved to me. It is my contention that this was one wonderful lady. If she had been visiting purely as a duty and not from the heart she wouldn't have turned round at each door and waved as she did. Colin's final word on the visit was, 'Dad I feel so proud that the future Queen of England (which she was then) should spare time to visit me.'

God bless her, in Heaven now, with Colin.

Some while after ministering to Colin and his friend Willem in the Netherlands – and conducting Colin's funeral – Ron Thomlinson wrote an article entitled 'A Theology that Isolates' for the June 1992 issue of *The Officer* magazine, a magazine that goes to Salvation Army officers throughout the world. Here, too, is a very moving account that I quote with slight adaptation for the purposes of this book:

It was a few days before his friend, Colin, died that Willem rang me. We had never met before and he had been given my number by the staff of our goodwill centre in Amsterdam.
'My friend is an Englishman, who has come to Holland to die,' he began. 'When it happens, would you conduct his funeral service?'
Of course I would, so I said to him:
'Willem, if I am going to bury your friend, I would like to meet him before he dies. It is so impersonal conducting the funeral of someone you don't know and perhaps I might be able to offer you both some help'. So we met, prayed together and read from God's word. Willem's friend, Colin, had planned his funeral service right down to the last detail. Rarely have I seen two people so much in love and rarely have I seen such caring. Willem made huge financial and emotional sacrifices for the friend whom he loved so much.
Within days of the telephone call, and our subsequent meeting, the funeral service had taken place. At the crematorium, the sight of Willem mourning his friend visibly moved even the hardened stewards, who see several funerals a day. As you might expect, we prayed together, thought about some Bible verses and listened to several songs, including 'Somewhere Over the Rainbow' sung by Judy Garland; 'Unchained Melody' by The Righteous Brothers; and Barbara Streisand singing 'Somewhere'.
Willem's friend had died as a result of Aids and was a gay man. A great number of those present at the funeral were gay. How they needed to hear those words of comfort that only Jesus can speak to people who mourn!
Just like everyone else!
Since then I have had continuing contact with Willem. Sometimes we drink coffee together, talk and pray. When he is very upset, he lets me into his world. He is so lonely. For the first time in his life he had known, with his friend who is now dead, what it was like to be complete in a relationship.
I am not thinking here about the promiscuous gay man, who is just as out of line as is the promiscuous straight person. This

91

relationship was so different from that. It was the loneliness and the isolation of the gay man that hit me most and I couldn't help but think we are in danger of propagating a theology that isolates gay people even further from our Christian circles.

It is worse when we consider that our understanding of God's ways should not lead to the promotion of anyone's loneliness. But gay witch-hunting certainly does that. The cliché about 'loving the sinner but hating the sin' seems so inexplicable and remote from the reality of life that it is an insult to hurl it around in this matter of being gay. What do such clichés mean anyway and how do you separate the two?

But this situation is the same for all those unable to express their sexuality in a socially acceptable or 'Christian' manner. What about the sexuality of the physically and mentally disabled; the single; the bereaved; the divorced? Are their sex drives suddenly dammed up so that they play no further role in their lives? We sometimes show as little understanding for such situations as for the person who is gay.

If you're happily married you're all right. If not, too bad. Only the happily married are allowed to express their sexuality.

In the spring of 1978, when I was 33 years old, my wife died and I became a widower. I was looking through some secondhand books for sale outside a rather cheap-and-nasty shop in south London. There were all kinds of books in the cardboard boxes and, standing beside me, was a middle-aged man, who looked just as unhappy as I was feeling. He was flicking through the pages of a paperback. It was a pornographic novel, with sex as its theme, and I understood perfectly well his need to read it. I wanted to read it myself.

Jesus' hardest and most scathing words were not for those caught up in the trap of their own sexuality. Whilst not condoning their actions, he was kind to them. He was bitterly angry with the heartless, loveless religious leaders who, cost what it may, wanted everyone to keep to the rules, even though they knew it was impossible.

Jesus hated religious hypocrisy. We have turned his values upside down. We reserve judgment on bad spiritual leadership, condoning it by our silence. And we crucify those who are unable to express their sexuality in a way that is acceptable to us.

I like to think I know how Jesus would talk with Willem – but how could I make Willem feel spiritually at home in my church?

How indeed?

24.

Positional Statements

THE focus of my ministry has been the pastoral and practical support of people living with Aids, their friends and families. This is also the main focus of this book. As such ministry has occasionally given rise to queries about the Army's stance in regard to gay and lesbian people, it may be helpful if I express a few points. I say occasionally because the main focus of people living with Aids is dealing with a potentially life threatening illness.

A person may become an adherent of the Army, in which case they look to the local Army and its officers for spiritual ministry and regard the Army as their church.

Those wishing to become more deeply committed as members – soldiers – study the Army's eleven doctrines of faith. These are in line with the main beliefs of most denominations of the Christian Church. In addition, they consider principles of the Army regarding their conduct as members. If after consideration they agree with these things, they sign a document and are publicly enrolled.

Positional statements on moral and social issues reflect the general teaching of the Army but are not binding upon the consciences of individual members, not least because such individuals have not appended their names to the statements. In other words the Army does not put members into straightjackets in regard to their thinking. In addition, positional statements are revised from time to time. These points are summed up in a statement, approved by the General in June 1996, which should accompany positional statements:

> A positional statement indicates the consensus and corporate view of The Salvation Army on a given topic as at the date of issue. All statements are subject to periodic review. They represent the official position of the Army and therefore an officer's teaching and counsel should be consistent with them. However, acceptance of their contents is not a condition of membership of the Army, and so the positional statements ought not to be regarded as an attempt to bind the consciences of individual Salvationists.

So how are positional statements formulated? For many years the Chief of the Staff established ad hoc groups to consider subjects and draft positional statements. These were brought to the General's Advisory Council for further consideration and recommendation to the General. However, in 1987 an International Moral and Social Issues Council was established and I became a member in 1989. The council's role included drafting positional statements and making recommendations in regard to subjects on which leadership would appreciate the council's thinking. In the early 1990s the international council ceased and became the United Kingdom Moral and Social Issues Council. Other countries were urged to establish their own councils and some took the opportunity to do so.

The United Kingdom council comprises officers and lay members, representing a variety of skills and interests. It meets four times a year, including a residential conference. For an urgent or particularly complicated issue, a working group can be convened to deal with the subject. Generally speaking, my judgment has been carried by contents of positional statements, although occasionally I have not agreed with every point. It would be a sad world if we all thought alike!

The positional statement on homosexuality has over the years been revised a number of times. The latest statement is, in my opinion, the most understanding. A few years ago, I was asked if it was time to again revise the statement. I advised against this for several reasons. A revision would have been too soon after the previous statement and people might tend to think the Army did not know its mind on the matter. In addition, I considered there needed to be more time for internal debate on the issue. Changes in international leadership, which would need to approve the statement, made it diplomatically unwise at the time.

Positional statements are comparatively brief, though they often deal with complex and contentious issues. They are not easily drafted. It may take a year or more before a final proposal is made to leadership. Nor does the Army issue a statement on every subject that may be requested. People wishing to see the Army's positional statements on a variety of subjects may go on the internet to www.salvationarmy.org.uk then click on 'quick links' and choose 'positional statements'. Or write to:

The Chairman, Moral and Social Issues Council,
The Salvation Army,
101 Newington Causeway,
London SE1 6BN.

On some issues there are diverse opinions both within the Moral and Social Issues Council and within the Army as a whole. I personally consider this point should be incorporated in some positional statements.

25.

Exclusive or Inclusive?

IN South London, some years ago, I noticed a Christian denomination that described itself on its church noticeboard as 'Strict and Exclusive'. Doubtless, members of the church were sincere and good people but I found the words off-putting, sensing that even as a Christian I would not be welcome into such an exclusive company. As a result, I had no aspiration to attend that place of worship.

I'm concerned lest within the Church as a whole, the Army included, we develop a tendency to become exclusive rather than inclusive. We see it happening in political parties, when a particular group will seek to gain the ascendancy to the exclusion of others, perhaps the majority, who may vary from them in regard to party policy. All too often such groups are very vocal, dogmatic and uncompromising in their agendas, even in the Church.

Early influences in my Christian experience led me to value the inclusive rather than exclusive nature of the Christian faith. The fundamental truth lies in such verses as John 3:14-16 – which I deliberately quote from the *King James Version*, the version which influenced me in my youth:

> As Moses lifted up the serpent in the wilderness, even so must the Son of man be lifted up: that whosoever believeth in him should not perish, but have eternal life. For God so loved the world, that he gave his only begotten Son, that whosoever believeth in him should not perish, but have everlasting life.

The word 'whosoever' is used twice in that short statement. In Sunday school and adult services we frequently sang the words of Philip Paul Bliss, found in *The Song Book of The Salvation Army* :

Whosoever heareth! shout, shout the sound;
Send the blessèd tidings all the world around;
Spread the joyful news wherever man is found;
Whosoever will may come.

My ministry to people affected by Aids has been an inclusive ministry, a ministry for the 'whosoever', otherwise I would have been given short shrift!

Allan was a smashing chap. In his basement flat, approached down steep steps, he always made me welcome, taking pride in showing me the small back garden he was seeking to improve. Though far distant, his family was supportive, as were some good friends. In those early years there was limited life expectancy and I became concerned when Allan was admitted to Westminster Hospital. Though poorly, we both agreed he would be okay and that I should go away on a weekend appointment and see him on my return.

To my dismay and sorrow, he took a turn for the worse and died while I was away.

Family and friends urged me to conduct Allan's funeral. The service took place in the Blantyre Street Salvation Army hall, Chelsea. It was quite remarkable to see the hall crammed with the family plus a host of predominantly gay men. They all needed the consolations of the Christian faith just as much as each other. Afterwards we went to the upper room of The Coleherne public house, where Allan and his friends had downed many pints. An excellent buffet was provided free of charge by the management, with drinks available for purchase.

Everyone had, in a sense, been in my territory at the Army. Now I was in theirs and in this more relaxed setting I was able to converse at greater length with family and friends. For me, it was an inclusive event that enhanced the effectiveness of my ministry.

When helping the family deal with Allan's possessions, I was given Allan's bonsai tree which now has a place of honour in the entrance porch of my home. Visitors look quizzically at the bonsai, wondering if it is real or not. I have to admit it was made by one of Allan's relations! Nevertheless it looks good and is a pleasing reminder of a fine friend.

I have always held Catherine Baird in high esteem. Originating from Australia, she spent her formative years in South Africa, transferred as a Salvation Army officer to the United States of America then finally to England, where she retired in the Balham district of London.

In his book *Pen of Flame – The Life and Poetry of Catherine Baird* John C. Izzard, states:

> As the years took their toll, Catherine spoke of her friends at the launderette and in the Balham community, many of whom were years older than she, while reflecting on her old age. 'I must delve into a deeper search for the truth about God, revealed in Jesus Christ my Lord.. . . . This has made me relinquish the foolish attempt to shape everybody into one mould. The gardener would tell me not to try changing roses into tulips, or violets into pansies. As I began to learn in District Six (in Cape Town, South Africa), I must love unconditionally.'

The words of Catherine Baird find an echo in my own heart and experience, confirming the gospel as I understood it from my youth – that the gospel is for the 'whosoever'.

Sometimes it's not been necessary to know a great deal about a person in order to establish a deep bond of trust and friendship. Simply facing the reality of living with Aids has been enough.

So it was with Jack.

The nurses at Westminster Hospital suggested I visit Jack, a 23-year-old from America, who was going through a difficult time. I sensed he'd had a difficult life and now, far from his original home, he faced the daunting prospect of the illness. When I took General Eva Burrows with me one afternoon, visiting people with Aids, she was kind enough to go to see Jack in his side room of the ward. This thrilled him immensely, particularly as she spoke of her visits to his homeland.

Jack was quite poorly, so was transferred to the residential unit of the London Lighthouse, where he continued to receive tender loving care from medical staff. I bought him a pair of boots, as it pained him to walk and these somewhat eased the pain. Whenever he saw me from the end of the corridor, he would shout 'Trevor!' and stride towards me and give a bear hug. He gave and received a lot of love from everyone associated with him.

I visited him almost every day and he was soon on the telephone if, rarely, I missed a day! A sudden deterioration in health necessitated his return to Westminster Hospital. I was determined he should not die alone, so to ease pressure on me good friends from the Lighthouse worked out a rota for night and day. Apart from two short breaks, I was with him for the whole of the last night and then, at dawn, a friend arrived to take over while I went to my office.

Soon after my departure dear Jack peacefully died.

Jack's mother had written him just prior to his death. She was not in the best of health and was undergoing surgery. Her postscript says it all:

You're my son and I love you no matter what.

I still picture that young man, Jack, in my mind, striding towards me with arms outstretched in anticipation of a loving embrace. As with so many others, he has a special place in my heart.

I'm reminded of years of service in Scotland, where I often heard the saying 'We're aa Jock Tamson's bairns'. Writing for *Leopard* – The Magazine for North-east Scotland, Wilma Thompson suggests the origins of that phrase. A relation of hers, John Thomson, was born in 1787 and became an innkeeper in Usan, a fishing village south of Montrose. Responding to an inquiry after someone in the village, one of his daughters remarked 'Naebody here o' that name, we're aa Jock Tamson's bairns.' It is possible that either the father or the daughter is the originator of the phrase. On the other hand, the Duddingston Kirk history suggests that the parishioners of the respected minister, the Reverend John Thompson, gave rise to the saying.

Whatever the truth of the matter, it can act as a reminder that we are all God's children, known and loved by him. I am confident that the Almighty knows all there is to know about Jack and that he opened his arms wide, so to speak, in a loving embrace. I am reminded of Fanny Crosby's song, with the first verse and chorus:

> Jesus, keep me near the cross;
> There a precious fountain,
> Free to all, a healing stream,
> Flows from Calvary's mountain.

> *In the cross, in the cross, be my glory ever;*
> *Till my raptured soul shall find rest beyond the river.*

(*Salvation Army Song Book*, 115)

26.

Touched by a Loving Hand

SINCE long before the film version swept the board at the Oscars, I have thoroughly enjoyed the writings of J. R. R. Tolkien, particularly his epic *The Lord of the Rings*. My old box of cassette recordings of the serial on BBC radio, broadcast some years ago, has been loaned to a number of friends. At the point in the story where Merry and Faramir are facing death, we read:

> Then an old wife, Ioreth, the eldest of the women who served in that house, looking on the fair face of Faramir, wept, for all the people loved him. And she said:
> 'Alas! If he should die. Would that there were kings in Gondor, as there were once upon a time, they say! For it is said in old lore: The hands of the king are the hands of a healer. And so the rightful king could ever be known.'
> And Gandalf, who stood by, said:
> 'Men may long remember your words, Ioreth! For there is hope in them. Maybe a king has indeed returned to Gondor.'

I have often remembered that passage when I've prayed to the Almighty, pleading that his healing touch might find even the likes of me as a conduit for his grace.

It came to mind all the more when the media picked up on the fact that Diana, Princess of Wales, was visiting and actually holding the hands of people who had Aids. Her actions contrasted sharply with the harsh tones of many voices, including those of some within the churches. She was saying, 'It's okay, it's safe to do so, it's good to care.' This generous public gesture, which we now take so much for granted, reminds me of another Crosby hymn, with the verse:

99

Down in the human heart, crushed by the tempter,
   Feelings lie buried that grace can restore;
Touched by a loving hand, wakened by kindness,
   Chords that were broken will vibrate once more.

Some years ago in India, I became acutely aware of the reactions of fear and prejudice produced by leprosy. At one hospital I visited, there was a fine, upright, good-looking young man, who had been a leprosy patient but was now healed. 'Why is he back in hospital?' I asked. Back came the reply, 'Because, though healed, when he went back home his father was so fearful that he took his son and threw him into a bonfire, hence the severe burns on his body.'

In the early years of the Aids pandemic, a comparison with people who have leprosy would hardly be exact, but there were things in common, not least fear and prejudice. Growing public awareness of Aids and increased education has, thankfully, reduced such reactions in these present times.

Thinking of how our Lord socialised and had mercy on the so-called outcasts of his day, including people with leprosy, Mona Westergaard writes of his compassion in her poem *The Touch*:

He stood alone, apart from the crowd,
His leprous flesh a concealing shroud
For longings stifled and joys outworn,
Forgotten laughter and hope stillborn.

Many who saw that shrunken figure -
Arrogant in their health and vigour –
Gathered their moral robes around them,
Self-righteous in the code which bound them;

And looking down their legal noses
They quoted from the law of Moses:
And prating of inherited sin
Saw naught of the tortured soul within

Which, outwardly to its fate resigned
Craved still the company of its kind –
The longed-for sound of a once-loved voice,
And friendships that made the heart rejoice.

Could they not tell – they who knew so much –
How great his need of a human touch?
But Jesus sensed it. Along the way
Many sought him for healing that day,

But, seeing the leper standing there,
Eloquent in his wordless despair,
He drew aside from those who clutched Him,
And stretching forth his hand – he touched him.

Mona Westergaard

Philip was not the sort to suffer fools gladly.

He was a professional man, used to giving people instructions. Chosen to present Diana, Princess of Wales, with a bouquet when she officially opened the Kobler Centre, attached to the Chelsea & Westminster Hospital, he gave the lashing of his tongue to the authorities when an official inadvertently divulged his surname to the media.

Philip was one of many people prepared to be 'up front' in order to educate people and dispel ignorance and fear. He had agreed to give interviews to the media in those early years of the mid-eighties, but was careful to lay down conditions – and woe betide anyone who betrayed his trust!

I thanked God for Church leaders, who in those early years were not averse to visiting people with Aids and setting an example to people in the pews.

I recall how deeply touched Philip was by a visit from his own church leader, the Archbishop of Canterbury, Dr Robert

At the opening of the Kobler Centre

101

Runcie. Sitting on the bed, holding Philip's hand, he chatted at length and gave him his blessing.

Philip was not too proud to accept fresh fruit, which used to be collected by my colleagues at our centre in Chelsea. Those were years when State benefits were very reduced and there was need for good food and nourishment.

Philip lived in a bedsit, maintaining it in immaculate manner, in one of the high rise blocks overlooking the River Thames. Some of the media gave the impression that these flats were 'riddled with people with Aids' but Philip and I knew of only two! He was kind enough to permit me to bring General Eva Burrows into his flat to converse with him.

Shane, a nurse from the Charing Cross Hospital Medical School was also invited into Philip's flat to meet the General. Prepared to appear in the media and express his views on euthanasia, Shane also had met Diana, Princess of Wales, when he was a patient in Mildmay Mission Hospital.

Michael, whose story is related in the chapter 'A Case In Point' was also with us, as a member of Body Positive and as a former member of the Army. The men readily responded to the General's engaging personality, only a little unease being evident when she touched on the subject of homosexuality. On this occasion, however, her concern for people with Aids in this and other lands was palpable.

Robin Bryant's photograph is a pleasing reminder of the occasion and of three men who were up front about their illness and who, by this means, touched the lives of many people, allaying fear and prejudice.

27.

Prayer in Action

MEMORY is a strange thing. It's said that everyone over a certain age can remember exactly where they were and what they were doing on 22 November 1963, when President Kennedy was assassinated. One of my most vivid memories is of hearing the Army's Chief of the Staff, Norman F. Duggins, preaching in Paisley, Scotland, in 1961. I was sitting behind the speaker, in the second row on the platform, next to Frank Hutchins, Duggins's private secretary. Having finished his sermon, Duggins collapsed, was rushed to hospital and died.

I'm not good at remembering sermons – a testimony to my own bad memory rather than the worth of sermons! But I've always remembered Duggins' sermon, with its three main points – National Altars, Family Altars, Personal Altars. It's good to have one – an altar. And by that I don't necessarily mean a physical altar, though that may be important for some people. As the hymn writer, John Oxenham, suggests, it may be a quiet place to which we resort:

> A little shrine of quietness,
> All sacred to thyself,
> Where thou shalt all my soul possess,
> And I may find myself.
>
> *John Oxenham*

The well-known writer on holiness, Samuel Logan Brengle, used to advise having a mercy seat within the heart, there to kneel in prayer in one's mind's eye in time of need.

We each have to devise what is best as individuals. Personally, perhaps because of my reserved nature, I find spontaneous public prayer difficult – I would rather give a sermon! I marvel at the flow of language when some people pray in public. I just worry a little that some will not be heard 'for their much speaking' (Matthew 6:7, *KJV*)! For me, *private* prayer comes more naturally. And I don't mean just when kneeling in my home but also when communing with the Almighty when walking in the Cotswold Hills, or when driving the car.

Jesus sometimes had to catch the moment. On one occasion he was confronted with a man who was deaf, had a stammer and pleaded for healing. We read:

> And he took him aside from the multitude, and put his fingers in his ears, and he spat and touched his tongue. Then, looking up to heaven, he sighed, and said to him, 'Ephphatha', that is, 'Be opened.'
>
> (Mark 7:33-34, *NKJV*).

No use kneeling in prayer in those circumstances, the upward glance of the eye was sufficient to intimate prayer.

Don't interfere

Years ago, during a lunch break, I nipped into St George's Tron Church, just off George Square, Glasgow, for a brief period of quietness and prayer. On the far side I saw a woman sitting in a pew, quietly weeping in prayer. My 'Salvation Army officer instinct' was to go over and ask if I could be of help. Then a voice within said, 'Trevor, don't worry, she's in the right place, she knows who she's talking with, so don't interfere.' That incident often comes to mind when I see people quietly praying in hospital chapels.

Prayer, even in private, is not always easy. Deep within one's being there is a well of thought and emotion, which cannot be put into words, and one must allow the Spirit of God to fathom those depths. As James Montgomery says in his hymn:

> Prayer is the soul's sincere desire
> Uttered or unexpressed,
> The motion of a hidden fire
> That trembles in the breast.
>
> *James Montgomery*

Day by day – and night by night! – I was involved alongside nurses in the care of Dennis. Seeing me one evening, nurse Francoise Greening, a Religious Franciscan Sister, remarked, 'Trevor, I'm going off on retreat with my order, the Franciscan Missionaries of Divine Motherhood. I want you to know I'll be praying for you and Dennis.'

At a time when emotions were very tender, those words of assurance came as answered prayer from one even greater, who said:

'Lo, I am with you alway, even unto the end of the world.'

(Matthew 28:20, *KJV*).

For a hospital chaplain, the occasional visit to a patient may merit a prayer, or communion, or the patient may attend the hospital chapel for a service. For me, when I am often continually in the presence of those with whom I am personally involved, constant prayers would be inappropriate. Better not to suffer from prayer indigestion! I give the assurance and people know I am privately upholding them in prayer.

Personal experience

Lacking many of the embracing round of services and other spiritual exercises enjoyed by colleagues in other appointments, because ministry is so very much 'out there' in the community, there has been all the more need to be heedful of personal experience. This is expressed in a prayer worked into a sampler in the nineteenth century, which was once in the possession of the Community of the Resurrection of our Lord, in Africa:

Lean Hard

Child of my love, lean hard,
And let me feel the pressure of thy care.
I know thy burden, child, I shaped it,
Poised it in mine own hand;
Made no proportion
Between its weight and thine unaided strength;
For even as I laid it on, I said,
'I shall be near, and while she leans on me,
This burden shall be mine, not hers:
So shall I keep my child
Within the encircling arms of my own love.'
Here lay it down nor fear
To impose it on a shoulder which upholds
The government of worlds.
Yet closer come!
Thou art not near enough.
I would embrace thy care.
Thou lovest me! I know it. Doubt not then,
But, loving me, lean hard.

105

Helpful prayers can be culled from a variety of sources. When participating in the funeral service of a friend who was a Jew, I became aware of the following prayer from the Jewish tradition. Rabbi Larry Tabick tells me it is named *Ne'ilah* and is in the final service held at dusk on Yom Kippur, the Day of Atonement, the holiest day of the Jewish year.

I quote the prayer in full, although only the latter part was used during the funeral service:

> The day is fading, the sun has set. Our Father in Heaven, quieten the doubts that rise within us, and our inner confusion, so that peace may find its way into our hearts and there make its home – your peace which comes as we forgive others, and you forgive us.
>
> Soon we shall journey from this house of prayer to our homes. May this peace we have sought here through our prayers and fasting return home with us, so that our homes can stand firm in life's storms, sheltering all that is generous and good in us from all that is mean and false.
>
> For yet another home you have prepared for us, when our time on earth has ended: an eternal home more sure than all the earthly homes that we have known. The stars will soon appear in the dusk. Be our guiding star as we journey into life everlasting. And as the gates of this world close, open again the Gates of Mercy for us, and we shall enter in.[1]

Likewise from the Roman Catholic tradition comes this prayer of faith:

> Go forth upon thy journey from this world, O Christian soul,
>   In the peace of him in whom thou hast believed,
>   In the name of God the Father, who created thee,
>   In the name of Jesus Christ who suffered for thee,
>   In the name of the Holy Spirit, who strengthened thee.
> May angels and archangels,
> And all the armies of the heavenly host,
>   Come to meet thee.
> May all the saints of God
>   Welcome thee.
> May thy portion this day be in gladness and peace.
>   Thy dwelling in Paradise.
> Go forth upon thy journey, O Christian soul.

[1.] Forms of Prayer for Jewish Worship edited by the Assembly of Rabbis of the Reform Synagogues of Great Britain, Volume 3, Prayers for the High Holy Days, 8th Edition 1985, published by Reform Synagogues of Great Britain, The Sternberg Centre for Judaism, 80 East End Road, London N3 2SY.

Father Damien was a priest who ministered to people with leprosy, eventually contracting the illness himself. The prayer, *Known,* by Charles K. Robinson, used by the Damien Ministries, has a sense of intimacy:

I know you.
I created you.
I am creating you.
I have loved you from your mother's womb.
You have fled, as you now know, from my love.
But I love you nevertheless and not the less and, however far you flee, it is I who sustain your very power of fleeing, and I will never finally let you go.
I accept you as you are.
You are forgiven.
I know all your sufferings.
I have always known them.
Far beyond your understanding, when you suffer, I suffer.
I also know all of the little tricks by which you try to hide the ugliness you have made of your life from yourself and others.
But you are beautiful.
You are beautiful more deeply within than you can see.
You are beautiful because you yourself, in the unique one that only you are, reflect already something of the beauty of my holiness in a way which shall never end.
You are beautiful also because I, and I alone, see the beauty you shall become. Through the transforming power of my love you shall become perfectly beautiful.
You shall become perfectly beautiful in a uniquely irreplaceable way, which neither you nor I will work out alone.
For we shall work it out together.

In contrast my friend, Michael, was much moved by his visit to Iona, where in AD 563 St Columba founded a monastery and his missionaries spread Christianity throughout Scotland. There with the present day Iona Community, Michael learned to value such prayers as:

Deep peace of the running wave to you,
Deep peace of the flowing air to you,
Deep peace of the quiet earth to you,
Deep peace of the shining stars to you,
Deep peace of the Son of peace to you.

28.

Suicide

URING the days of National Service, it was common to see servicemen hitch-hiking. My mother would chide my father if he passed a serviceman and failed to give him a lift. Following family tradition, I have enjoyed giving lifts and have met many interesting people. When I was secretary to William Leed, the Army's leader in Scotland, he encouraged me to do this. One day we gave a lift to two Germans, Karl and Ernst, who were hitch-hiking in the Highlands. This contact resulted in them later staying at my parents' home in Gloucestershire for several days! Nowadays, of course, greater caution is exercised, particularly in view of dangerous incidents experienced by some people.

More recently I saw Pierre, standing beside the westbound side of the A40, by Hanger Lane, drenched in the pouring rain. I pulled up, he got in the car, and I took him all the way to Cheltenham, which was, coincidentally, the destination of both of us. We retained contact and I later gave him another lift, concluding the journey with a meal at my parents' home. Pierre had a pleasant personality and I was pleased when one day he said that he and his girlfriend were going to Greece on holiday. While camping, they were set upon by a group of men, so they immediately returned to London, badly shaken. Pierre was particularly affected and one day his girlfriend arrived at his flat to find he had taken an overdose of tablets and killed himself. Shocked, I wondered if I could have done more to be supportive.

At least I was able to minister to his mother.

Since that experience, Aids ministry has confronted me with the subject, as some of the people with whom I have been involved have attempted suicide and I have had to rush them to hospital. By and large, young men do not easily resort to suicide but, faced with the daunting prospect of a life-threatening illness, particularly in the early years of the pandemic when hope for the future was considerably diminished, it was understandable.

I was very much involved in the support of David, who was all too conscious of his declining health. He knew I would respond immediately, in response to his telephone call, and rush him to Charing Cross Hospital when he attempted suicide. I had a key for his flat, so was able to let myself in and bring this about. But care of the body was just one part of the story.

Responding to David's wishes, arrangements were made for me to take him to Aylesford Priory, near Maidstone, for a week's respite break. As it states in their publicity leaflet:

> The Carmelite Friars and a team of lay helpers offer hospitality as a way of serving God and neighbour.

I thanked God for such a ministry. There David had a single room but was able to share fellowship with other guests at mealtime; he could enjoy walks in the lovely surroundings; and if there was need for counselling or attendance at services of worship this was available. I still have a vase from the Aylesford Priory pottery that David bought for me while there. A week later, when I took him back to London, he was very much refreshed physically, mentally and spiritually.

The 1995 Health of the Young Nation Conference, convened by the Department of Health and held in the Queen Elizabeth II Conference Centre, London, highlighted among other things the Government's aim to reduce the number of suicides, especially in the younger age group. The event was chaired by Jon Snow. Virginia Bottomley, then Secretary of State for Health, addressed the conference, as did other well known people.

Dr Lorraine Sherr, Consultant Clinical Psychologist and Senior Lecturer at the Royal Free Hospital School of Medicine, prepared the report *Suicide issues in a cohort of HIV positive clinic attenders – A case note audit study for the Health Education Authority*. In 1994 the doctor's colleague, Barbara Winstone, had invited me to the hospital for interview in connection with the study. It was an opportunity to reflect on my own experiences of pastoral care for people who have attempted suicide.

In January 1996, the London Lighthouse convened a conference entitled *Suicide and Self-harm*, that again highlighted the problems we were facing, particularly in the early years of the pandemic. For those of us involved with people who have attempted suicide it is an anxious time, all the more distressing if they are comparatively young in years and the bond of friendship is strong. Spending hours in hospital with them, sometimes through the night, and just being there can be vitally important. It's not so much what is said or done but rather just being there, perhaps just holding their hand is important. It assures them that someone cares – and God cares!

In the words of John Gowans's song in *The Salvation Army Song Book:*

> Someone cares, someone cares,
> Someone knows your deepest need, your burden shares;
> Someone cares, someone cares,
> God himself will hear the whisper of your prayers.

Before and After –
Advance planning for death and funeral arrangements

(ISBN 0854126260)

Advance planning for death and funeral arrangements.

by Trevor A. Smith

PHOTO BY DAVID (see pages 44,113)

J. H. Kenyon, the funeral directors of Kensington, sponsored 10,000 copies of this publication.

Though born out of Aids ministry, the booklet is applicable to most people.

A few copies are still available from:

Wandsworth Oasis
Trading Company,
547 Battersea Park Rd
London SW11 3BL

or

The Salvation Army
Social Services
101 Newington
Causeway
London SE1 6BN.

(Price £1 to cover post/administration)

29.

Where There's a Will

I WAS always glad to visit Paul and he was appreciative of visits, as was his partner, Brian, who had a strong personality and was very supportive of his ailing friend. They loved each other deeply.

As health declined, there was very much need for care. Acute night sweats that would soak the bedding, vomiting and diarrhoea gave rise to additional washing and ironing in order to keep pace with everything. At times I felt heartsore for Paul when he related how he had ventured out shopping, only to have an 'accident' and needed to return home. The sense of uncleanness and stench, caused by the diarrhoea, was abhorrent to him. He had such a lovely personality and bore it all with dignity and stoicism.

I took Paul and Brian to the seaside, to Sheerness, where they enjoyed a 'break away from it all,' and my snapshots reflect their happiness.

Paul had such a lot with which to cope. He came from a small village, where everyone knows everyone else, so being gay was all the more difficult, particularly when at church he heard the minister strongly denounce homosexuals. It drove him away from the church and the community. He loved his mother and other members of the family and the last thing he wanted to do was to hurt them. He was therefore not open about his sexuality, about having a partner, and now about having Aids.

As the family lived far from London, I had not previously met them. When Paul was admitted to hospital, seriously ill, his mother came and had to come to terms all at once with the fact that, even though she may have known it in her heart, her son was gay, had a partner, and was terminally ill. This lovely mother broke down in tears in my arms.

The minister at the local London church conducted a helpful funeral service, appreciated by the few of us present – the family as is the custom

111

sitting in the front pews. What grieved me was that Brian, the partner, was not mentioned in the service and was obliged to sit at the rear of the church, not at the front beside the family. It may be that the minister was not fully aware of the circumstances. I vowed never to allow that to happen in any service I conducted.

Thankfully, the majority of families, who have been aware of the circumstances, have been supportive of relations who have been ill with Aids, considerate towards gay partners and friends, and anxious ultimately to fulfil the wishes of their loved ones. The vast majority of gay men with whom I have associated in my ministry have placed a high value on family life and have appreciated the support of parents, brothers, sisters and other relations.

A not inconsiderable number, however, have had problems. For understandable reasons there have been times when it has been necessary not to mention Aids, either in conversation or in funeral services. Sometimes, however, such confidentiality is misplaced, enforced due to family relationship problems. The word 'circumspect' has been described as like a cat walking carefully along the top of a wall into which splinters of glass have been embedded.

How often have I had to walk circumspectly!

Sensitive to the living

When conducting funerals, it is vital to respect the wishes of the deceased, yet be sensitive to the attitudes of the living, particularly the families. Funeral director, Barry Albin-Dyer says in his book *Don't Drop the Coffin!* (Hodder & Stoughton ISBN 0340786647):

> Allowing the family to have a say in the way a funeral is conducted does make life more difficult. But I could see that by inviting the family to make decisions over the kind of funeral they wanted for their loved one, the day would be that extra bit special and those present would remember it for many years to come.
> The role of the funeral director is primarily to work with the living, not the dead.

It's to the credit of Barry and his colleagues in the Bermondsey company of F. A. Albin & Sons that the funeral arrangements of one of my best friends, John, passed off smoothly and memorably. Barry's book *Don't Drop the Coffin!* has since been read with interest and the television series prompted by the book was viewed with fascination.

Sometimes it has been necessary to conduct the funeral service at the crematorium, after which the family has departed, duty done. With family gone, the partner and friends can breathe a sigh of relief, relax and enjoy the reception afterwards, where they may speak freely and with appreciation of all that the deceased meant to them. In such circumstances, I have often thought how much the family missed out.

Occasionally, whether in the heterosexual or the gay community, there are times when families gather around relations who are terminally ill. They may not have been supportive in the past but now 'blood is thicker than water' – or is it? Perhaps I have become cynical in old age and am unimpressed by 'crocodile tears', knowing full well they want to give the impression of loving care but have eyes on the possessions of the relation, sometimes earmarking them even before they have died.

Before and after

As already stated, the majority of families are supportive. They seek to fulfil the loved one's wishes, including being supportive of the friends and partner, if there is one. Alas, however, for those where the relationship of the friends and partner is not recognised, when a will has not been made! The family may claim the lot. It is difficult for older people to contemplate making out wills and for the younger age group the very thought of making a will is repellant.

It was for these reasons and more that, when an ecumenical group met for discussion in premises nearby St Cuthbert's Church, Earls Court, I was urged to write a booklet giving guidelines. This resulted in the publication of *Before and After – Advance planning for death and funeral arrangements* (see page 110). Though born out of Aids ministry, the booklet is applicable to most people and many people with cancer, or caring for people with other illnesses, have purchased copies from Wandsworth Oasis Trading Company, or from The Salvation Army. David, a former director of the Aids organisation Frontliners, with whom I was involved as friend and carer, took the attractive front cover photograph.

It was during this period that there was extended correspondence with Charlotta Schlyter of the Centre of Medical Law & Ethics, from King's College, London. A joint project being developed with the Terrence Higgins Trust had resulted in a consultative process with a number of interested parties. It was intended to publish what came to be called an

Advance Directive, more commonly known as a *Living Will*. In contrast to a normal will, it does not deal with possessions, and does not at present have any legal force. It does, however, aid a doctor in consultation with loved ones to conclude how a patient would wish to be treated in the event that, perhaps through mental incapacity, they are unable to make an informed decision.

In fact on the front page of the form it states:

NOTE TO DOCTORS: THIS LIVING WILL IS NOT A SUBSTITUTE FOR DISCUSSION.

On his own initiative, David completed a form, stating that if an indication of his wishes was needed it was stated in the form that I was to act on his behalf in consultation with the doctor. Thankfully, there was no need to enact the requirements but the form was there if the need arose. I was glad David had completed a normal will, which dealt with possessions, even if as executor I was landed with a lot of work!

Sensitive items

On a few occasions when fulfilling the role of executor I have had cause to dispose of sensitive items, such as condoms, in order to avoid embarrassment for mothers. There has also been the need to shred sensitive diaries, where a person has sometimes written at length about their sorrows, hurts and joys. I also have faced a dilemma when dealing with responses to a 'lonely heart' advert. If the people knew the person who had advertised had died, they might wonder what had happened to their photographs and brief write-ups about themselves. I decided that the best thing to do was to return the documents with a kindly covering letter explaining the circumstances.

I've occasionally helped people draft their wills but have preferred to refer them to experts in this field, such as a solicitor or a Terrence Higgins Trust representative. Nick, who originated from my home county of Gloucestershire and who was up front about his illness, had an article in the magazine *Positive Nation* in which he says:

> The Salvation Army has helped me do my will and sort out all the paperwork and the staff in the Mildmay and the Trinity Hospice have been wonderful. They're all pretty sensitive about what's going on.

Experience prompts me to urge everyone to make out a will when they are in good health and able to focus their attention on the subject, rather than wait until severe illness suggests the wisdom of doing so but when a 'turn for the worse' can sometimes make it too late.

30.

Know your Limits

OVER the years I have gladly conducted services at Army places of worship throughout the country. It has been an enjoyable ministry, particularly if it has brought encouragement to smaller centres of activity. Young people at such places often feel themselves isolated and lacking in peer support, so encouragement to them is particularly crucial.

However, as involvement in the care of people with Aids increased, it entailed devoting more time to this ministry, resulting in additional stress factors. So it was agreed with superiors that I would be wise to reduce the number of services conducted. A case of prioritising.

Some people skilled in Aids ministry have travelled the length of the country, sometimes going overseas, lecturing on the subject and leading seminars, and there has been the danger of burnout. The policy was therefore adopted that whenever a colleague wanted someone to lecture on the subject of Aids they would be urged to take advantage of local people skilled in this sphere. This seemed sensible, as it facilitated the establishing of relationships with a view to mutual support in the future, whereas if I were to visit it could be more in the nature of hit-and-run tactics.

For me, as a coping mechanism, a good stint of gardening, a brisk walk round the block, or a walk over the Cotswold Hills when opportunity permits, works wonders. Then, too, the companionship of good friends, in whose company I can relax without necessarily talking about work, is a real bonus.

There was a period of concern for nurses at Mildmay Mission Hospital. Many terminally ill patients were dying. This had an undoubted effect on nurses, as they were mostly in the same age group.

Steps were taken to ensure all staff had access to counselling, if they so desired. Some wisely took advantage of this provision. Others preferred to go as a group to the local pub or restaurant for a drink and a chat.

In the words of Charles Wesley:

> Help us to help each other, Lord,
> Each other's cross to bear;
> Let each his friendly aid afford,
> And feel his brother's care.

And I guess it's equally true of sister's care!

Each individual has to cope in the way that suits them best, not as someone else dictates. The important thing is to know one's limits, both physical and in other respects, and work within them.

There are, indeed, limits to what one can cope with. At a time when Army leadership was concerned about my workload, a colleague, Marjory Parrott, expressed a conviction that she should become increasingly involved in Aids ministry. Marjory was a God-send. A very industrious person, she quickly became involved, becoming a part-time chaplain at Mildmay Mission Hospital, chaplain to Chalk Farm Oasis, a carer for ACET, and also involved with CARA and Grandmas. Representatives of all these voluntary organisations and more speak highly of her ministry and we were all sorry when the time came for her to move to pastures new, this time appointed with John to serve in the Czech Republic.

Doubtless Marjory could write a book about her ministry!

Minister and carer

I have advised anyone contemplating becoming involved in Aids pastoral ministry to consider a crucial point. It may be sufficient to be involved with people, without exception, simply as a minister of religion. If exceptions are made, it may be possible to combine the rolls of minister of religion and carer. But this will inevitably entail more demands on time and emotion. Both roles entail a degree of friendship. In some instances, the two roles may be joined by the role of being a personal friend but such a commitment in Aids ministry has obvious cost, as will be realised in reading this book.

The Salvation Army song 'Christ is All', written by Herbert Booth, was a favourite of Michael, and my emotions are moved whenever it is sung. The last two verses express acknowledgement of limitations yet confidence in God:

I've little strength to call my own,
And what I've done, before thy throne
   I here confess, is small;
But on thy strength, O God, I lean,
And through the blood that makes me clean,
   Thou art my all in all.

No tempest can my courage shake,
My love for thee no pain can take,
   No fear my heart appal;
And where I cannot see I'll trust,
For then I know thou surely must
   Be still my all in all.

Herbert Booth

I've had to be careful to maintain the focus of my ministry – pastoral support of people affected by HIV/Aids. There have been times when some people have encouraged me to also become involved in other issues but, had I done so, this would have undermined my main focus. I have also sought to confine myself to issues relevant to my membership of the Army's Moral and Social Issues Council.

Easily contracted

I also had to safeguard my ministry in other ways. A friend contracted hepatitis A. We surmised it was by means of contaminated seafood that he had enjoyed. As he was very poorly, it resulted in me being all the more involved in his household chores, such as doing his washing and supporting him also when admitted to St Thomas's Hospital. I somehow picked up the infection, perhaps by a lapse in standard hygiene practice. As a consequence, after he had recovered to a marked degree and was at home again, I became very poorly. My skin and eyes competed with amber traffic lights!

The acute illness had to take its course, there being little that can be done except take care of one's self and try to recuperate. It resulted in a visit to the Lloyd Clinic at Guy's Hospital for blood tests and immunisation against hepatitis B. It was a learning experience. I learned that as a healthcare worker I should already have been immunised against hepatitis B, as it is so easily contracted. Even the British Dental Association published a booklet that page by page makes a comparison between HIV and hepatitis B, showing the infinitely greater risk of contracting the latter.

The experience proved useful in more ways than one. I readily made it known that I had hepatitis A, lest anyone think I had contracted HIV. What a cause for gossip that would be! Such awareness proved useful when a worker in one of our hostels contracted hepatitis A and needed advice from leadership. A further outcome was that when the Army's *Quality Standards Manual* was revised, colleagues took advantage of my experience and the subject was dealt with, the recommendation being that people staffing such places as hostels should voluntarily seek immunisation against hepatitis B.

It's often possible to turn bad experiences to good account. After all, the Bible says:

> All things work together for good to them that love God, to them who are the called according to his purpose
>
> (Romans 8:28, *KJV*).

And that 'all' I have taken to mean even the adverse experiences of life.

31.

Holy Communion

TOGETHER with other friends, Philip and I were glad to accept the invitation to attend St Botolph-Without-Aldgate for the ordination as minister in the Church of England of our friend Nurse Pat Wright. At that time, Pat was a nurse in Mildmay Mission Hospital, so she brought with her a team of supporters.

We were at the front, as Philip was in a wheelchair. The Bishop of London conducted the service, including the ordination, followed by Holy Communion. We made a beeline to Pat to be among the first to receive communion from her. Those were times when the ordination of women was still a contentious issue within the Church of England but we were proud to be supportive of Pat.

The sacrament of Holy Communion, in its varied forms, has meant much to some of the people with whom I have been involved. When the Aids organisation, Body Positive, held its annual service in St Cuthbert's Church, Earls Court, opportunity was given for people to take Holy Communion in a side chapel.

A friend of mine, John, appreciated Holy Communion, not least when a patient in Guy's Hospital, retaining and letting me have the order of service used by the chaplain. Others, too, have appreciated such a ministry.

While the Army does not practise the outward form of the sacrament of Holy Communion, it does in its services seek to emphasise the inward nature of the experience that the symbols represent.

The Army is not opposed to Holy Communion and any member of the Army is at liberty to partake of the sacrament when ministered elsewhere. Indeed, in certain circumstances an officer may administer communion. I recall William Leed telling me that when in Australia it came to his turn in an ecumenical group to administer Holy Communion, he did not hesitate to do so.

But, as I say, the Army emphasises the inward nature of the experience of communion. When Albert Mingay, at that time leader of the Army's work in Scotland, attended the Nottingham Faith & Order Conference of the British Council of Churches, each denomination was invited to conduct a service after the style of their respective denomination.

He conducted a typical Army holiness meeting, using what some have termed the Army's Holy Communion song written by Albert Orsborn, and often sung to the tune of 'Spohr':

> My life must be Christ's broken bread,
>   My love his outpoured wine,
> A cup o'erfilled, a table spread
>   Beneath his name and sign,
> That other souls, refreshed and fed,
>   May share his life through mine.
>
> My all is in the Master's hands
>   For him to bless and break;
> Beyond the brook his winepress stands
>   And thence my way I take,
> Resolved the whole of love's demands
>   To give, for his dear sake.
>
> Lord, let me share that grace of thine
>   Wherewith thou didst sustain
> The burden of the fruitful vine,
>   The gift of buried grain.
> Who dies with thee, O Word divine,
>   Shall rise and live again.

Albert Orsborn

Michael loved to go on pilgrimage to the island of Iona, off the north-west coast of Scotland, where in AD 563 St Columba founded a monastery, his missionaries spreading the Christian faith throughout Scotland. While there, Michael purchased and used Holy Communion vessels, which I now keep in remembrance of him.

PHOTO BY KERRY

Kevin

Kevin was a smashing chap. He was up front about his illness and became a member of the Aids organisation Frontliners. Manning the Frontliners' office in Mildmay Mission Hospital, he felt somewhat isolated from the head office in the city.

Nevertheless he did good work in seeking to be supportive of patients and staff, relations and friends.

I would invariably call on him when at the hospital.

Time came when he became a patient in Mildmay, so his friends Chuck and Kerry and I continued to spend time with him. We were each aware of Kevin's declining health, yet he remained strong in spirit and in full control of his life.

Though in a very weak state, Kevin requested Chuck and Kerry to prepare a meal for the four of us in the ward day room.

Visitors had the liberty, in those times, of preparing some meals in the ward kitchen. So the four of us sat down to a superb meal and really good fellowship, bound together in a common bond of seeking to be supportive of Kevin.

We knew in our hearts that it was unlikely we would have such a meal together again. It was as if Kevin was deliberately bringing us together for this Last Supper and it was indeed a veritable Holy Communion. I sensed another presence and the blessing of God upon us in that unique moment. These are treasured memories of a fine man, beloved by his mother and friends, who still maintain contact with me.

Grant

Grant was a gentleman of style, a handsome fellow with a flamboyant personality. People warmed to him. As a ballet star, he was used to centre stage and whether socialising in a restaurant, or associating with friends elsewhere, his engaging personality drew the attention of people like a magnet. One sensed he was still centre stage even when in failing health.

Grant's life had not been without sorrow. Lora, the attractive young lady he had hoped to marry, died of cancer, so Grant willingly and lovingly took responsibility for the wellbeing of her teenage daughter, Tamara. His life was enriched as he saw her growing into womanhood.

I first met Grant in St Stephen's Hospital, where he was diagnosed as having Leishmaniasis. Trust Grant to have an exotic illness!

The doctors and nurses who had cared for him in St Stephen's and Westminster Hospitals, and also at home, had a special place in his heart. They had seen him in his most vulnerable dependent state – not an easy experience for a proud independent young man. He was considerate towards them and others.

When he was a patient in a side room of the Robert Hudson Ward, Grant seized a large glass jar. Making a hole in the metal lid and labelling the jar, he begged money from everyone visiting him, eventually raising sufficient to purchase a new washing machine for the ward. It was his way of saying thank you.

He was even considerate to birds, of the feathered variety! His room had a casement window overlooking the hospital grounds, in which he could see them. He was delighted when at his request I purchased a nut dispenser to hang outside his window, enabling him to watch the blue tits feeding. He had little sympathy with the pigeons!

It was always a pleasure to visit his Mayfair flat and then, later, the Chelsea flat. More than that, an invitation to stay at his rented Cotswold cottage, in company with his friends Nicholas and Caroline, enabled me to see Grant from yet another perspective, for here was a place which refreshed his whole being.

Grant was sensitive to spiritual things and deeply appreciated the Holy Communion service in Westminster Hospital and also on other occasions receiving Holy Communion at the hands of Father Bill Kirkpatrick. Bill and I were with Grant on his last day. Talking in anticipation of his funeral, he remarked, 'It should be a lovely day out for everybody!' and he knew in so saying that he was leader of the day, the focus of attention, that he was still centre stage.

What style to conclude his last day, his life, by remaining fully alert all day, sat up in bed and chatting with friends and sharing in champagne drinks in the evening, sipping it off a spoon, while candles burned around us.

It sometimes struck me as quite remarkable that I got on so well with Grant. He had an extrovert personality, was a socialite and a scintillating conversationalist, whereas I was the opposite.

I had never been to a ballet performance, but Grant stimulated my interest, resulting in me taking two women nurses to see the Christmas performance of *The Nutcracker* performed in the Royal Festival Hall. It was a memorable experience. My regret is that I did not know Grant in better times and see this gentleman of style perform centre stage in ballet.

32.

A Case in Point

'MOTHER will skin me alive,' said Michael when visiting my Curtis Street office, Belfast. In an escapade with other young teenage lads, he had lost his shoes, so a visit to a nearby shoe shop resolved the matter. Those were tough times for Michael's parents, his sisters and brothers, not helped by 'the Troubles' that were at their height in the period that included 1973. After meeting him at the Army in Shankhill, I visited the family in their terraced home, just off the Shankhill Road.

As a young member of the Army, he had learned to play the trombone – an asset for years to come. But the foundations of his faith were also laid and continued to develop through the years, proving their worth in troubled times ahead.

Though having university potential, he was obliged to conclude his education and seek employment. A number of jobs followed, even an attempt to enter the Navy. His frustration with life in Belfast, particularly some people's bigotry, prompted him to join The Royal Irish Rangers as a musician, resulting in him being stationed in Germany. Later receiving an honourable discharge, he came to London, where after a period in a hostel he took up residence in a flat in Mary Jones House, overlooking the Army's Riverside House hostel. I wonder if the residents knew a 'spy' was so near!

Michael worked for a company in Hackney, and also participated in the Army's activities in Barking, giving a hand with young people's work and valuing friendship, worship and participation in the band.

Michael had always been good at writing letters, often debating issues, as evidence my bulky files of correspondence. Such letters reflect increasing trust and confidence and his progress in faith and human experience.

Writing in 1977, he says:

> Trevor, I am going to tell you a very personal thing. After you have read it, I'm afraid you will in so many words tell me to go to hell or something to that effect.... Shucks, I may as well tell you. I am a homosexual and have been completely aware of the fact since I was sixteen. Call me 'queer', 'bent', whatever you like – I'm as God made me. Awful to the ears of a Christian and I am sorry if it offends you but, Trevor, that's me.'

As the years unfolded, Michael became increasingly open about his sexuality and, no, I didn't tell him to 'go to hell'. After all, there are gay men and lesbian women in the Army, some of whom are married, most of whom do not divulge their sexuality. It is how they conduct themselves in behaviour that matters.

When a member of the Army at Barking, Michael wanted to have David as a partner and live with him. He knew at that time it was against the requirements of membership as a 'soldier' of the Army, so debated the matter with me in correspondence and conversation. Wanting to be completely open, Michael discussed the matter with the leaders of the Army in Barking and it is to their credit that they were understanding and helpful. As a consequence, out of principle, Michael left the Army with great reluctance but without bitterness. The uniform of which he was so proud was worn no more.

Together with his partner, Michael became a member of the Metropolitan Community Church, which at that time had premises in Sistova Road, Balham, and was led by the Reverend Jean White. Here he felt comfortable as the church readily accepted lesbian and gay people, many of whom wished to be open about their sexuality and have partners.

The denomination was founded by the Reverend Troy D. Perry in 1968 in Los Angeles. The Reverend Freda Smith, formerly an active member of The Salvation Army, became one of its outstanding leaders. Although Michael had at one time expressed an interest in becoming a Salvation Army officer, this was not to be, so instead he studied and eventually became a minister in the church.

He had become HIV positive and due to advancing symptoms, was obliged to give up work. He therefore studied at the University of Greenwich Avery Hill Campus, gaining a Bachelor of Arts degree in theological studies. This in spite of contending with his illness and being in hospital for a period with meningitis!

While studying, Michael undertook a community work placement at the Church Army home in Putney. The report by the person in charge gives a graphic view of Michael's qualities:

Michael has proved to be a deeply caring and sensitive person, whose work has been very much appreciated at Leinster Lodge. He has been involved in most of the daily practical duties involved in caring for the elderly within a residential setting. Duties have included helping residents with mobility, serving food, washing dishes, leading worship in the home's chapel and spending time with residents. In this respect he has shown initiative, one example being arranging for a resident to receive a visit from the Estonian Embassy. This contact will be maintained, especially as the resident speaks mainly Estonian, with little English. He has contributed well in the home's daily report sessions. With regard to strengths and weaknesses, Michael's strength is his sensitive care and understanding specially demonstrated in his relationships with staff and residents. He identified one of his major weaknesses as his inability to say 'no' to people who may be over-demanding but says he is improving in this respect.

Following this achievement, Michael studied and gained a Master of Theology degree at King's College, London. His theses for this period give an insight into his depth of thought and experience. He had indeed proved he had university potential!

Michael was a member of the Aids organisation Body Positive, among other things taking it in turn to man the telephone helpline. Having this and other experience as a person living with Aids, I invited him to accompany General Eva Burrows when I took her on a visit to people with Aids.

On another occasion, Michael accompanied me on a flight to the Isle of Man, where his parents at that time resided. At the invitation of George Davison, Nursing Officer at the Noble's Isle of Man Hospital, we spoke on the subject of Aids to the nurses in the lecture theatre. We both enjoyed time with Michael's family and, yes, driving in the family car along part of the route taken by the TT races.

Increasingly I transported Michael from his home in Rotherhithe across London to see Dr Ken McLean, Lead Consultant in GU Medicine at the Charing Cross Hospital, who had originally met him in 1986. Michael not only trusted and had confidence in Ken's medical skills but also regarded him as another friend, someone in whom he could confide.

In 2003 there was a naming and dedication gathering in which I was involved to mark the naming of the Charing Cross Hospital clinic as The Nkosi Johnson Unit. Nkosi was the 11-year-old Zulu boy who gave his testimony as a person living with Aids at the International Conference on Aids, held in South Africa, and who made such a worldwide impact on television. Sadly, he died soon after.

His foster mother, Gail Johnson, was present. She spoke at the ceremony and unveiled a portrait of Nkosi. Dr John Wright, who had worked in South Africa, undertook organising the event, ably supported by Dr

PHOTO: ROBIN BRYANT

Michael

Ken McLean and colleagues, both doctors addressing the gathering.

When visiting a friend in Germany, Michael received a call to urgently visit his mother, who was now living in Wakefield and had become terminally ill. Alas, he was not in time to see her before she died. He had also become ill and was admitted to hospital in Manchester, where he knew a number of friends in the city. Thankfully he was well enough to be released for his mother's funeral, which I conducted at the Army hall in Wakefield. The service ended, Michael gave me a thumbs up, so I must have done something right!

Having chatted with him in the family home, I returned to London, little realising his health would rapidly deteriorate and he died in April 1997. Together with several friends, I went to Manchester for his funeral service conducted by the Reverend Hazel Addy in the Blackley Crematorium. As Dr Ken McLean states in a letter, 'I was immensely fond of Michael and it caused me much grief that he died when we had almost achieved viral suppression. It was so strange that his final illness happened when he was out of London, depriving me at least of any direct contact at that time.'

It was agreed with his friends and the leaders of the Metropolitan Community Church that I should conduct Michael's memorial service in the church that latterly had been his spiritual home. Featured on the front of the order of service was a photograph of Michael, taken while on a visit to Iona, an island and community he loved so much.

Metropolitan Community Church leaders both here and overseas sent messages for the occasion and these were read to the crowded church. There was also a message from the Reverend Malcolm Johnson of St Martin-in-the-Fields, who among other things stated:

> His books, which are being given to his old college, King's in The Strand, betray the width and depth of his interests – theology, philosophy, poetry, literature and liturgy.

PHOTO: ROBIN BRYANT

Michael in degree robes

With the death of Michael I lost a very good friend. In addition, the Army lost an able person, someone who wanted to be open about his sexuality, including the fact that he desired a one-to-one relationship with a partner.

He decided on principle to leave the Army. But God did not desert him! Indeed, God's grace was increasingly evident in his life.

In browsing through Michael's rough lecture notes I came upon a statement that says it all:

Think! God chose the foolish – look at me!!!

Epilogue

AGED just 18, I rose early as the sun was rising and the dew was on the grass, made my way out of the garden gate half way up Leckhampton Hill and, nearing the summit, paused at a large boulder near the track. There in the quietness of the early morning I knelt and responded with a sincere 'Yes' to God's call to enter the ministry through The Salvation Army. I made the decision publicly known when attending the evening service later that day.

Next day my call-up papers for 'National Service' in the Royal Air Force arrived. Possibly I could have been excused on grounds of entering the ministry but I thought the experience would be good and test my convictions. So as a sprog – service slang for a new recruit – I wended my way to Cardington to be kitted out and then to Bridgnorth for basic training, thankful for the Salvation Army Red Shield club on camp that provided fellowship and refreshments. Then to Warton, near Blackpool, for medic training, little realising how God was even in those days preparing me for the future. There followed a brief period at Moreton-in-Marsh and then the remaining long period at Hornchurch where service personnel and their families were treated in the Sick Quarters. On Sundays, it seemed funny to go in and out of the camp in my Salvation Army uniform and salute any passing RAF officer!

On discharge, and after a year in industry, I entered the Army's William Booth College, Denmark Hill, London, envisaging nothing other than ministering to a local congregation, having been inspired by the local leadership of Harold and Mrs Hobson, Elsie Janes and Betty Morgan. As it transpired, I was given only one such appointment, at Beeston, near Nottingham. Thereafter I was given a variety of admin appointments, all of them adding to experience, latterly being head of department, from which emerged the appointment as Director of Aids Support Services.

I've certainly had cause to praise God for his leadership in my life and the fact that he can use even the likes of me in ministry to other people.

Recently, I again strolled on the hill, the pace somewhat slower than in my youth, but there the boulder remains, weathered by the storms of the years but still firm. Somehow it reflected the spiritual journey and caused me to be thankful for all experiences, including ministering to people affected by HIV and Aids.

It prompted another word of prayer. Something along the lines of the following prayer that you may wish to share as it seems so appropriate for the age in which we live. Written by Arch R. Wiggins, it is number 529 in *The Song Book of The Salvation Army* and can be sung to the lovely tune of 'Finlandia'.

> Thou art the way, none other dare I follow;
> Thou art the truth, and thou hast made me free;
> Thou art the life, the hope of my tomorrow;
> Thou art the Christ who died for me.
> This is my creed, that 'mid earth's sin and sorrow,
> My life may guide men unto thee.
>
> Hold thou my feet, let there be no returning,
> Along the path which thou hast bid me tread;
> Train thou my mind, I would be ever learning
> The better way thy fame to spread;
> Keep thou my heart ablaze with holy burning
> That love for souls may ne'er be dead.
>
> I would bring peace to lives now torn asunder,
> Ease aching hearts with words that soothe and heal;
> I would bring peace when, breaking like the thunder,
> Men rise in war, and hatred feel.
> Peacemaker, Lord! Now I am stirred to wonder;
> O take me, and my calling seal!
>
> *Arch R. Wiggins*